LAMINATED DESIGNS IN WOOD

LAMINATED DESIGNS IN WOOD

TECHNIQUES • PATTERNS • PROJECTS

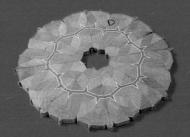

Clarence Rannefeld

LARK
BOOKS

Asheville, North Carolina

To my readers, in the hope that they receive as much pleasure and inspiration from reading the book and putting some of its methods into practice as I received from developing the technology and writing the book.

EDITOR:
Laura Dover Doran

BOOK AND COVER DESIGN:
Chris Bryant

ILLUSTRATIONS:
Clarence Rannefeld

PHOTOGRAPHY, FINISHED PIECES:
Evan Bracken,
Light Reflections, Hendersonville, NC

PHOTOGRAPHY, PROCESS SHOTS:
Clarence Rannefeld

ILLUSTRATION ASSISTANT:
Bobby Gold

Library of Congress Cataloging-in-Publication Data
Rannefeld, Clarence.
    Laminated designs in wood : techniques, patterns, projects /
Clarence Rannefeld.— 1st ed.
        p.   cm.
    Includes index.
    ISBN 1-57990-021-6 (paper)
    1. Woodwork.   2. Laminated wood.   I. Title.
TT200.R36   1997
684'.08—dc21   97-25656
                                                            CIP

10 9 8 7 6 5 4 3 2

Published by Lark Books
50 College Street
Asheville, NC 28801
USA

© 1998, Clarence Rannefeld

For information about distribution in the U.S., Canada, the United
    Kingdom, Europe, and Asia, call Lark Books at 828-253-0467.

Distributed in Australia by Capricorn Link (Australia) Pty Ltd.,
    P.O. Box 6651, Baulkham Hills Business Centre, NSW 2153, Australia

Distributed in New Zealand by Southern Publishers Group.,
    22 Burleigh St., Grafton, Auckland, New Zealand

Printed in Hong Kong

ISBN 1-57990-021-6

CONTENTS

Acknowledgments

I GRATEFULLY ACKNOWLEDGE THE ASSISTANCE OF THE FOLLOWING:
Adelle (Del) Rannefeld, homemaker, loyally stood by me throughout the writing process and assisted me by making decisions, giving advice, offering helpful suggestions, and carefully editing the manuscript; David N. Rannefeld, math, science, and economics teacher, thoroughly checked the mathematical equations in chapter 9; David Winton, journalist, photographer, and public relations specialist, carefully edited the manuscript; Gary G. Rannefeld, industrial electrical engineer, inspired and patiently guided me through many problems I encountered in my attempt to become computer-wise; and James W. Rannefeld, furniture designer and manufacturer and woodworking teacher, made the only mitered laminate I had ever seen before I started working on the process.

Also, for generously returning gifts to be pictured in this book, I am grateful to Dr. and Mrs. Arthur B. Beindorff (bowl, page 80; candle box, page 120 [right]), Mr. and Mrs. Julian L. Bibb, Jr. (bowl, page 66; cutting board, page 102), Mr. and Mrs. Richard L. Leonard (bowl, page 102; lidded jar, page 11; clock, page 121), Mrs. Robert C. Agee (candle box, page 120 [left]; clock, page 19), Mrs. Charles Bradley (candle box, page 117), Mr. and Mrs. David Neely Rannefeld (tray, page 79), and Mr. and Mrs. Quilla D. Reed (tray, page 66; cutting board, page 115). The cutting board on page 19 [top center] was made by James Walter Rannefeld.

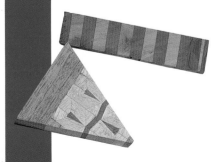

Preface

THE PRIMARY FOCUS OF THIS BOOK IS *DESIGN*. A design is a graphic representation that is consciously arranged to produce a particular result or effect. Designs have been an integral part of the history of civilization and have played an important role in the development of human culture. Artistic designs are often the trademark of a civilization—each culture has its own styles, which are different from those of other cultures. Most designs are symbolic, representing a feature, attribute, virtue, characteristic, deity, or mood. Ancient designs were handed down from generation to generation over thousands of years. These designs are the fingerprints of a culture and allow archaeologists to classify even a tiny shard.

We come in contact with many examples of visual designs every day in drawings, paintings, sculptures, and architecture. Designs are used to decorate buildings, homes and home furnishings, and many other consumer products. Fabrics, wallpaper, bedding and linens, tableware, flooring, furniture, draperies, and toys are just a few of the many things that are enhanced or decorated with designs. These include designs that have their origin in antiquity as well as designs made or developed in more recent times.

An important element of many designs is repetition. Often, lines, shapes, and colors are repeated throughout a design. (This is true of the designs in this book.) Another principal of design is harmony or balance. Both symmetrical or asymmetrical designs can be pleasing to the eye. In fact, designs that exhibit contrasting or discordant elements of design can be quite appealing. There is unity when a design contains more of one element than any other. For example, a design made up primarily of one color has a certain sense of unity.

Professionals generally agree that most designs fit into one of four categories: fine arts, graphic arts, decorative arts, or useful arts. Painting, drawing, and sculpture are considered fine art. Graphic arts include engraving, printing, photography, and bookmaking. If a design is used primarily to enhance something—a case, shelf, or coffee table, for example—it is classified as decorative art. A cutting board used as a wall hanging or a box displayed in a case would be considered decorative art. If, however, a decorative item is used in some functional or practical way, it would be considered useful art—for example a cutting board that is used to cut bread. Thus, a mitered laminate design can be either decorative or useful, depending on how it is used.

It is my interest in design that has led me to develop the mitered laminates in this book. These designs were produced by the repetition of a simple process, with each repetition resulting in a new set of unique designs. In this process, there are only four variables to consider: the composition of the stripe, which can have thousands of combinations; the cutting location or where the laminate is cut into cross sections; the cutting angle, which is a continuous variable; and the orientation and positioning of the cross sections when they are glued back together. By altering these variables, it is possible to produce an unlimited number of unique designs.

Making laminate designs by repeating a standard procedure is a new concept. When I began this craft, I was able to find only a small number of mitered laminate designs, and there was no indication that there was a definite procedural link between these designs or that they were the results of a common and encompassing process. The designs that appeared in the books I read were mostly used to decorate wooden objects that were turned on a lathe, such as bowls, plates, vases, and urns. (It is possible to turn such items on a lathe, because the design extends throughout the thickness of the wood and can thus be seen on both surfaces of the item.)

The first design I made was a simple one that I copied from one my nephew, a furniture designer and manufacturer, devised. His design was a linear, second-generation piece, measuring 30 inches (76 cm) long, 4 inches (10 cm) wide, and about 1 inch (2.5 cm) thick; it had a handle on one end. In my first project, the design ran from one end of a board to the other. From that beginning, I learned to create other designs as I changed variables in the procedure. I discovered that a change in any variable produced a different and unique design. Then I learned how to convert a simple design into a very different one by repeating the procedure I had used to make the first one. It then became obvious that the second design could be transformed into a third, the third into a fourth, and so forth.

Though my first designs were all linear ones, I eventually learned how to cut a linear design so that the design made a sharp turn when the two ends were fitted together in a different manner. In this way, a design could be made that ran around the periphery of a square, a rectangle, a hexagon, an octagon, and other similar shapes (see pages 127 and 132). After making angled designs, I began to create circular and oval designs. I did this by cutting a linear design into sectors or pie-shaped sections and fitting these into a circular pattern. If this circular pattern is turned into a plate, for example, the design encircles its center (see page 72).

After I learned to make designs in a planar configuration, I wanted to learn to convert a linear design into one that encircled a cylinder. For this, I cut a linear design into sections similar to barrel staves (page 73). When these sections were fitted together into a cylindrical shape, the design ran around the periphery of the cylinder. A cylinder of this type, when fitted with a bottom, can be turned into a bowl, vase, urn, or any other symmetrical object (page 78).

Up to this point, I had made only designs with wood. Then I began to wonder why my new designs could not be made with paper. Using paper and the same procedure, it became apparent that all the designs *could* be made with paper, by "gluing" the cut paper sections together with transparent tape. Then I learned how to make these designs with a computer, using a graphics program.

Thus, I had two alternative ways to produce a large variety of designs. The use of paper or a computer was much more economical in terms of materials and time. These two alternatives provided a simple means of making designs that could be affixed to almost any material or object, using a diversity of application methods. I discovered that these designs are available to anyone interested in enhancing or decorating consumer products and, thus, afford many opportunities for people in fields other than woodworking.

In this book, I discuss two important aspects of these designs: production and application. With wood, these two are integrated; the design is developed as the process is carried out. In other applications, the design must first be created so that it can then be applied to the product as a second step or procedure. This realization made me understand the importance of the design itself.

The development of the design in wood as the process is carried out utilizes technology inherent in the wood-processing industry. Although the process is simple, it does require a knowledge of very precise techniques; guidelines for how to develop the necessary skills for mitered laminate work are detailed in this book.

Application of these designs on materials or products other than wood is usually a three-step process. The first step is creating the design by using the paper method or a computer. In the second step, the design is configured according to the procedure outlined in this book. Third, the design is applied to the product or material. In the third step, the necessary techniques and skills are generally the same as the ones used or practiced in the industry in which the design is to be applied. Thus, only a minimum amount of new technology or skills has to be learned to apply the designs to materials other than wood. See chapter 11 for detailed information.

Although many of the procedures and techniques described in the book are new and written primarily for woodworkers, most also have application in other pursuits and industries. It is my belief that mitered laminate designs will not only interest the amateur (or semiprofessional) woodworker and crafter, but also have far-reaching possibilities in design development in a wide variety of industries.

Summary of Book

The 12 chapters in this book cover all aspects of mitered laminate design. Chapter 1 is a general introduction to the book and the field. Mitered laminates are divided into two general groups, *standard* and *nonstandard*. Chapter 2 fully explains the process of making standard mitered laminates.

The standard process consists of four simple steps that produce a design from a laminated board or plank. The first step in the process is making a *linear laminate* or a strip(s) of wood sandwiched between two planks. In the next step, this laminate is cut into cross sections at an angle. In the third step, alternate cross sections are turned over. These are then glued together in step four, producing a *first-generation laminate*. This laminate can then be carried through the last three steps again to make a *second-generation laminate*. Then the process can be repeated as often as desired, with each conversion producing the next generation of laminates.

Chapter 3 discusses the technique required to make mitered laminates. This section includes information on how to fit small pieces of wood together into a design so accurately that it is difficult to detect the glue lines. All aspects of the process are described in detail, starting with making the linear laminate and ending with the final gluing process. It defines what criteria must be met to make perfectly joined and matched laminates and designs. Jigs that aid in making the laminates are described in detail, including information on how to make the jigs in your own shop—a procedure that requires only average woodworking skills.

Chapter 4 includes examples of the large number and wide variety of first-, second-, and third-generation designs that are made by cutting the cross sections at only three angles. The designs—three first-generation laminates, 27 second-generation laminates, and 162 third-generation laminates—are illustrated in this chapter.

Chapter 5 demonstrates the effects of certain variables on the laminate design: the complexity of the stripe in the linear laminate, the width of the cross sections cut from the laminate, the cutting angle of the laminate, the points at which the laminate is cut, and how the cross sections are glued together.

Chapter 6 details (with illustrations) how these planar laminate designs can be fashioned so that they have turned corners, thus creating angular, closed, circular, and elliptical designs. How these curved designs can be combined with linear forms to create designs that have any shape is also described. Planar laminates can also be cut and glued into cylindrical structures in which the designs run around the periphery of the cylinders. In this way, several designs can be combined into one object.

In the next chapter, chapter 7, a numbering system is described. I have devised this system in order to identify and classify mitered laminate designs. It is based on the process by which laminates are made and allows anyone to duplicate a laminate made by another woodworker simply by knowing this system.

Chapter 8 describes how to simulate the designs and patterns with paper or a computer. Using tracing paper and transparent tape to make patterns requires much less time and material than making designs with wood. The paper process permits anyone interested in creating designs to participate in this technique. How to use a computer to make designs is also illustrated and discussed.

To fit a design to a specific area, the final size of a design can be calculated before the project is committed to wood. The width of the cross sections (cut from the linear laminate) determines the final size of the laminate. Chapter 9 explains the exact relationships between the final design and the width of the cross sections cut from the linear laminate.

Chapter 10 presents several nonstandard procedures and the type of nonstandard laminates and designs these produce. This chapter illustrates the results when one step in the standard procedure is not followed, or when an additional procedure or step is performed on the laminate. Only a few of the many possible deviations from the standard are illustrated, but they open the door to many additional designs that can be explored by enterprising woodworkers—or anyone else with an interest in artistic expression.

Chapter 11 discusses the benefits of the mitered laminate process for various individuals and companies. The various products that can be enhanced with these designs and how these designs are applied are also listed.

When you get to chapter 12, you will be ready to put your knowledge of mitered laminates to work and create a beautiful design of your own. The last chapter gives detailed instructions for making five mitered laminate projects: a tray, a cheese board, a candle box, a clock, and a table.

The book contains a glossary of terms to use as a reference tool. Because this is a new field of work, new terms are needed to describe the technique. It's a good idea to review these before you read the book.

It is my hope that readers from many different fields of interests and with many different talents will enjoy this book. So as not to limit your creativity, areas in which more original and expanded work can be carried out are noted. The abundant uses for mitered laminate design are just being realized—so use your imagination and have fun!

C. E. R.

Chapter 1
Introduction

It's been my experience that most woodworkers, whether professional or amateur, are constantly looking for new ways to enhance and decorate wood. On the most basic level, this book addresses that need; it explores, in a step-by-step manner, methods that create a diversity of designs and patterns for creating beautiful wooden objects.

Most of this book is directed to the woodworker, but the techniques, methods, processes, designs, and patterns can be used by readers with diverse interests and talents. The designs are unique, intricate, artistic, and interesting, and they vary in scope, style, form, structure, and shape. The number of designs is virtually unlimited; many are still to be discovered. The designs can be created not only in wood, but in paper, fabrics, and other sheet materials.

There are many areas in which readers can pursue this technology, either as a profession or as a hobby. Quilters, pattern designers, floor- and wall-covering manufacturers, artists, and others can benefit greatly from this knowledge and can explore and expand the technology, either for their own use or in their field of work.

Why Laminate Wood?

What does the term *laminate* mean? Laminating is the process of gluing together layers of wood or other materials and using the finished product to make a variety of structures, forms, and shapes. Wood is often laminated when solid planks and boards are either unavailable or too expensive. Structural beams are made in this way. Parquet flooring, using small wood blocks to form geometric designs, is also made through a laminating process. In other industries, thin sections of wood are laminated into curved shapes that are very strong and stable; a tennis racket frame is an example of this technique.

Plywood manufacturers laminate to achieve strength and stability in two dimensions. In this industry, thin sheets of colored or printed plastic, which can be bonded to a rigid base, are called laminates. The base is medium-density fiberboard that can cover the top of a kitchen cabinet or be used as the sides, tops, and fronts of inexpensive furniture. Veneering (see page 12), which finds many applications in various industries, is also a form of laminating.

Laminating has also been used to achieve a visual or artistic effect by using the grain and color of the wood creatively. Each wood species normally can be seen on both surfaces of the laminate. By laminating different species of wood, the visual effect of the wood is enhanced, oftentimes resulting in attractive and artistic structures. Structures laminated in this way can be turned into circular shapes, such as bowls, vases, plates, goblets, spindles, or urns.

Laminating for Wood Enhancement

Several techniques have evolved over the years that produce decorated or enhanced objects in which the design goes all the way through the structure. The techniques involve gluing several wood pieces together in a variety of ways to make a patterned structure. Though many different processes are involved in making these, most of the processes can be grouped into one of four categories.

Traditionally, the method most often used is *blocking* (also called *layering* or *tiering*). In this method, square, rectangular, or flat stock is glued together in patterns to form planar rectangular shapes. These are then built up as layered or tiered stock by regluing the original or different layers together one or more times. These blocks are then sawed or turned into the desired shapes or structures. Many patterns can be made by using this method, and much work using this technique has been published and exhibited. Photos 1 and 2 show a simple example of this technique. (Note that both photos depict the same vessel.) This technique was also used in making the lidded jar in Photo 3 and the recipe card file box in Photo 4.

Photo 1. A BOWL TURNED FROM GLUED BLOCKS
OF WOOD FROM TEN UNKNOWN SPECIES;
6½ X 4 INCHES (16.5 X 10 CM)

Photo 2. THE BOWL VIEWED FROM ABOVE

Photo 3. LIDDED JAR MADE BY USING THE BLOCKING,
LAYERING, OR TIERING METHOD; 4 X 6½ INCHES
(10 X 16.5 CM); EIGHT UNKNOWN WOOD SPECIES

Photo 4. RECIPE CARD FILE BOX MADE BY USING THE
BLOCKING, LAYERING, OR TIERING METHOD; 6 X 4½ X 4½
INCHES (15 X 11.5 X 11.5 CM); OAK AND SILVER MAPLE

In another method, segments made of angular or mitered pieces, or straight or curved sectors, are glued into flat, circular, or cylindrical rings or stock. These can be used as is, or the flat rings and glued sectors can be stacked or tiered to form decorative turning blocks. This is the *segmented ring* method of laminating. Examples of this technique are shown in Photos 5 through 8.

Another laminating technique is the *band saw method* in which the design is produced from two species of wood slabs of contrasting color. The two woods are held together, one on top of the other, as the two slabs are cut simultaneously into the same pattern with a band saw. Then alternate pieces in the pattern are interchanged between the two woods. After the pieces are interchanged, they are glued back together, producing two patterns that are the same except with reversed colors. This procedure can then be repeated, producing a more intricate design.

The band saw method has found limited application. The saw kerf removes wood along the cutting line. Unless it is a straight cut, the curvature of the two cut edges will be slightly different. The amount of difference is proportional to the curvature of the cut. If the curvature is too large, the two cut pieces will not fit precisely when placed together. Plates made using this technique are shown in Photos 9 and 10 on page 15. The bowls in Photos 11 and 12 on the same page were also made using the band saw method.

The fourth method, *mitered laminate design,* is the one that will be fully explored and discussed in the following chapters. It is a simple procedure that can be duplicated over and over to produce an almost unlimited variety of designs. The process begins with a plank or board. The most decorative and artistic effects are achieved if the initial plank or board is made up of laminated pieces consisting of two or more species of wood.

The first step of this method consists of cutting the board or plank into cross sections at some angle less than 90°. These cross sections are then reassembled and glued together, forming a mitered laminated board. This board can be taken through the same procedure as above to form a second and different mitered laminated board.

This procedure can be repeated with the second mitered laminate, the third mitered laminate, and so forth.

At any stage in the procedure, the mitered laminated board can be used as flat stock or cut into segments or sectors. When glued back together, this produces circular stock for turning. The process is very simple, though the techniques require precision. The process and procedure are fully explained and explored in the following pages. An example of this technique is shown in Photo 13 on page 15. The hand mirror in Photos 14 and 15 on page 16 is another example of an item made with a mitered laminate design.

Mitered laminate design produces a design or pattern in the wood. The composition of the original laminate, the species of woods used, the widths of the laminated layers, and their arrangement and number are factors that determine how the final design or pattern looks. Another factor is how each section of the linear laminate is cut. Other factors are the width and the angle of these sections and how the sections are assembled. Variations of these factors result in different designs that enhance wooden objects of all types. This is an area that is of special interest to woodworkers, as it provides them with an additional means of enhancing their handiwork.

Other Wood-Enhancing Techniques

There are other methods of decorating wood surfaces that are often used to achieve similar results, such as veneering, marquetry, intarsia, parquetry, and inlaying. Veneering is the process of gluing very thin sheets of wood or *veneer* to a solid base for the purpose of enhancing its looks and value. Marquetry is the art of gluing very small pieces of different species of wood veneer to a solid base. The pieces of veneer are precisely cut to fit together to form a picture, design, or a scene. It is used to decorate furniture and make wall hangings.

In intarsia, a mosaic is made from small pieces of different wood species, which are inserted and glued into hollows or cut-outs in the surface of the base. Parquetry, used primarily for floors and furniture, consists of fitting pieces of wood together into a geometric or other pattern (as in parquet flooring). Inlaying is decorating the surface by inserting narrow strips of wood, usually of a different color or species, into a cut slot. It is used mainly for furniture.

Photo 5. A BOWL TURNED FROM TIERED LAYERS OF RINGS, EACH OF WHICH IS COMPOSED OF GLUED SECTORS; 9¾ X 6 INCHES (25 X 15 CM); WALNUT, MAHOGANY, AND THREE UNKNOWN WOOD SPECIES

Photo 6. VASE MADE BY USING THE SEGMENTED RING METHOD; 11 X 8 INCHES (28 X 20.5 CM); WALNUT, MAPLE, MAHOGANY, AND ONE UNKNOWN SPECIES

Photo 7. BOWL MADE BY USING THE SEGMENTED RING METHOD; 11½ X 5 INCHES (29 X 12.5 CM); WALNUT, MAPLE, CHERRY, AND BUBINGA

Photo 8. BOWL MADE WITH THE SEGMENTED RING METHOD; 9⅝ X 3 INCHES (24.6 X 7.5 CM); MAPLE, WALNUT, AND TWO UNKNOWN SPECIES

How does mitered lamination differ from these long-standing methods of decorating wood? One big difference is that enhanced mitered laminates have designs that go all the way through the wood. In veneering, marquetry, inlay, and other similar methods, the design goes only a very short distance below the surface. Also, in the laminating process, the design is the same on both faces of the wood. The design cannot be destroyed by removing the surface to any depth. For that reason, these enhanced mitered structures can be turned on the lathe without materially affecting the design itself.

Another distinction is the shape of the designs. The designs from mitered laminates have some limitations. They form only patterns with straight lines that change directions only at mitered corners; it is not possible to create true curved lines. Some designs come close to simulating curved patterns by using short pattern lines and small angles. In contrast, veneering, marquetry, or inlay can produce designs with both straight and curved lines.

Design repeatability is another difference between mitered laminates and veneering, marquetry, intarsia, or inlay. Designs can be and are repeated in the latter techniques, usually to achieve symmetry; however, it normally is not done for small areas. On the other hand, in making mitered laminates, it is the nature of the process to produce small designs or patterns repeatedly. In most cases, the designs are connected. Designs can also be made in which the stripe in one section does not connect to the stripe in the next one. Though these disconnected designs will be briefly explored (see chapter 10), the prime emphasis of this book will be on connected designs.

Designs for Any Configuration

You may wonder when and where mitered laminates designs can be used. Since the basic process produces a linear design or pattern that covers a long rectangular plane, the linear design can be made into many decorative objects that are flat or planar, and can be used to enhance breadboards, panels, wall hangings, trays, plaques, tabletops, and floors.

Instead of making a mitered laminate in which the design runs in a straight line, corners or simulated curves can be fashioned in the same plane. Geometric designs, circular designs, or combinations of the two, can be made to outline almost any shape: clock faces, round or oval picture frames, vessel bottoms, circular trays, plates, round plaques, circular tabletops, and shallow bowls.

Also, mitered laminate designs can be made to encircle spherical or cylindrical objects. Bowls, vases, urns, bottles, buckets, and other containers can be made with a band (or bands) encircling the periphery of the vessel. Thus, mitered laminates can be incorporated as a decorative motif into almost any object.

Other Applications

Later in the book (see chapter 8), I will explain how designs can be made with paper or a computer before committing the process to wood. This technique is quicker and much less costly and provides the woodworker with a knowledge of how the design will look beforehand. It also permits the woodworker to readily make changes in the design or process if required. Those who have access to a computer with a graphics program can easily generate designs.

Making mitered laminate designs with paper or on a computer is also of interest and benefit to nonwoodworkers. Professionals in industries that rely on the creation of new designs and patterns are constantly searching for new and appropriate designs for their goods. Many individuals, whether professional or amateur, are also interested in exploring and using new designs in their work. Professional designers and artists use designs and patterns for artistic expression in decorating works of art. This applies not only to their use of designs for their own creative endeavors, but also to designs that are produced for the benefit of manufacturers.

The new and abundant source of designs made possible by the mitered laminate process is useful to industries that rely on new designs and patterns to help market their products. There are several general methods for incorporating designs into or applying them to a manufactured product. One method is the use of a printing process to apply a design to the finished item. This could include such diverse products as printed laminates, textiles, plastic sheets, wallpaper, ceiling panels, interior decorating items, wearables, home accessories, paper products, rugs, draperies, bedding and linens, chinaware, or upholstered furniture.

Photo 9. A PLATE MADE BY THE BAND SAW METHOD IN WHICH TWO BOARDS OF CONTRASTING COLOR ARE CUT INTO PATTERNS TWICE AND REASSEMBLED EACH TIME BY GLUING TOGETHER ALTERNATING WOOD SPECIES; 16 X $\frac{7}{8}$ INCH (40.5 X 2.2 CM); REDWOOD AND YELLOW PINE

Photo 10. PLATE MADE BY USING THE BAND SAW METHOD; 13 X $\frac{7}{8}$ INCH (33 X 2.2 CM); REDWOOD AND YELLOW PINE

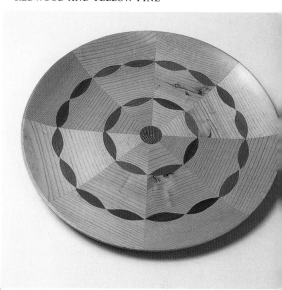

Photo 11. BOWL MADE BY USING THE BAND SAW METHOD; $14\frac{1}{2}$ X $5\frac{3}{4}$ INCHES (37 X 14.5 CM); POPLAR

Photo 12. BOWL MADE BY USING THE BAND SAW METHOD WITH DIFFERENT DESIGNS ON SIDES AND BOTTOM; $11\frac{1}{2}$ X $4\frac{3}{4}$ INCHES (29 X 12 CM); REDWOOD AND YELLOW PINE

Photo 13. A VASE IN WHICH THE TWO PERIPHERAL DESIGNS ARE MADE FROM THE SAME STANDARD MITERED LAMINATE; $7\frac{1}{2}$ X 12 INCHES (19 X 30.5 CM); MAHOGANY, WALNUT, AND MAPLE

One method is to combine the graphics elements in the starting material and to develop the design in the manufacturing process. Some products that could benefit from this method include wooden gift or decorative items, wood flooring, furniture, and architectural woodwork. Little or no modification would be required if the procedures in this book were used. A stripe would be incorporated in the starting material used for making the item and carried through the procedure to become part of the finished product.

Another method involves cutting out blocks or pieces of the design elements, fitting these together into a second design, then incorporating this aggregate into the finished product. A slight change to this procedure would be to fit and hold the various design parts together and, at the job site, fasten or bind the aggregate to a base or matrix. Alternatively, the design blocks or pieces could all be fitted together and secured at the job site.

In quilting, pattern sections could be cut out of different materials. Instead of gluing cross sections together, the quilt pieces or sections would be joined by sewing. This process could be used by the individual quilter as well as commercial establishments. Though there are some 4,000 documented quilt patterns, mitered laminate designs provide quilters with a much wider selection, in addition to an entirely different style of design.

For other products, the designs could be incorporated into the merchandise during the manufacturing process. This technique would apply to carpet manufacture and to fabrics made on the Jacquard loom or any similar machine.

My final suggestion for the use of mitered laminate designs is to cut out the parts of the pattern from different-colored materials, then fit and bind them together in several alternative ways. This is done at the job site to install countertops and vinyl and tile flooring. A much cheaper method would be to incorporate the pattern parts into the matrix during the manufacturing process.

Photos 14 and 15. HAND MIRROR WITH ONE FIRST-GENERATION AND ONE SECOND-GENERATION DESIGN MADE BY USING THE MITERED LAMINATE PROCESS; 5⅝ X 12 INCHES (14.1 X 30.5 CM); EIGHT UNKNOWN WOOD SPECIES

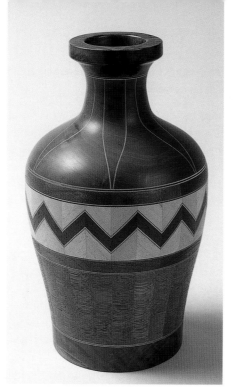

Photo 1. A VASE IN WHICH THE PERIPHERAL ZIGZAG DESIGN IS MADE FROM A FIRST-GENERATION MITERED LAMINATE; 5¾ X 10½ INCHES (14.5 X 27 CM); WALNUT, MAHOGANY, MAPLE, AND BUBINGA

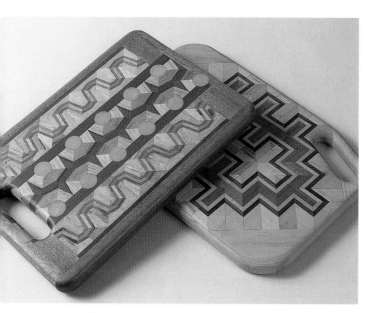

Photo 2. CUTTING BOARDS: (LEFT) MADE FROM TWO DIFFERENT SECOND-GENERATION MITERED LAMINATES, 15 X 10½ INCHES (38 X 27 CM), NINE UNKNOWN WOOD SPECIES; (RIGHT) CONTAINS BOTH A FIRST-GENERATION AND A SECOND-GENERATION MITERED LAMINATE DESIGN, 15¾ X 10½ INCHES (40 X 27 CM), MAPLE, WALNUT, AND CHERRY

Chapter 2
The Standard Procedure

Making mitered laminate designs is an essentially simple and straightforward process with many possible variations and combinations. This chapter will give an overview of mitered laminate designs produced under standard conditions. Later chapters will discuss how to deviate from these rules to create variations.

Standard and Nonstandard Laminates

A mitered laminate made by a set procedure and having specific characteristics is called a *standard mitered laminate*. It is made by using a set of standard variables. Any other laminate is designated as *nonstandard*; nonstandard laminates are covered in chapter 10.

A standard mitered laminate has the following characteristics:

1. The design is repeated.
2. At least one element of the design is continuous.
3. The design is symmetrical with respect to at least one axis.
4. The longitudinal axis of the design is perpendicular to the transverse axis.
5. The design extends throughout the thickness of the board.

A nonstandard laminate is different from the above in at least one aspect. If, in the process of making a mitered laminate, one step in the procedure is nonstandard, then the laminate produced is also nonstandard.

Standard First-Generation Laminates

The starting material from which all standard mitered laminates are made is a *standard linear laminate*. It consists of a "stripe" sandwiched between two boards called *outboard planks*. The outboard planks are of the same species of wood. The stripe is made up of an odd number of various wood strips. It can be composed of only one strip or of more than a dozen. If it is composed of more than one, all but the center strip must be added in matched pairs (same species of wood and same thickness). Each pair must be placed at the same distance from the center stripe, one on each side, making the stripe symmetrical along its longitudinal axis. A stripe made of five strips that forms a standard linear laminate is illustrated in Figure 1.

There are unlimited possibilities in making a standard linear laminate. Any number of strips of wood can be used, and the thickness of these strips can vary widely. The wood species used can also vary. The only requirement is that the stripe be symmetrical—the strips on one side of the longitudinal axis (center strip) must be a mirror image of those on the other side.

The second step in the process of making a standard mitered laminate is cutting the standard linear laminate into cross sections at an angle greater than 0° and less than 90°. For practical considerations, the range is normally between 15° and 75°. The width of the cross sections, also called *crosscut sections*, or *sections*, can vary from very thin to 2 or 3 inches (5 or 7.5 cm) wide.

One requirement in the production of a specific standard laminate is that all the cuts be made at the same angle. Another is that all of the cross sections be of the same width. The width of the sections cut from the linear laminate determines how large the design will be. The design from this step will have a zigzag shape. The angle of the cut governs how steep or flat the zigzag pattern will be. A specific section width and a specific cutting angle result in a specific zigzag design.

The third step involves turning every other cross section over or upside-down. If the stripe runs from the lower left corner to the upper right corner, turning it over results in the stripe running from the upper left corner to the lower right corner; or vice versa.

In the next step, the cross sections are glued together, resulting in a zigzag pattern. For a standard design, the stripe in each section must be matched to the stripe in the two adjoining sections. At least one element of the design must be a continuous stripe running from section to section. The result is a standard *first-generation laminate*. Photo 1 in this chapter (page 17) and Photos 6 and 9 in chapter 6 show examples of standard first-generation laminates.

Standard Second-Generation Laminates

A standard first-generation laminate is required for making a standard second-generation laminate. A second-generation laminate is made by repeating the last three steps above.

The zigzag laminate is cut into cross sections. As above, any cutting angle can be used; but for any laminate, all angles must be the same. However, there is a restriction on where the cuts can be made to produce a standard laminate—there are only two points through which the cuts can be made. One of these points, called an *A-point*, is at the exact center of a cross section design when the stripe goes from a lower position on the left to a higher one on the right. If the design goes in a direction opposite to this, or from a higher position on the left to a lower one on the right, it is called a *D-point*. Cuts can be made through either the A-points, the D-points, or both.

Following the procedure above, every other section is turned over. The stripe in each section is matched with the stripe in the two adjoining sections when the sections are glued together. These are standard second-generation mitered laminate designs. Thus at any angle, three different designs can be made from any first-generation laminate: one when the cuts are made through the A-points, one when they are made through the D-points, and one when cuts are made through both points.

The patterns resulting from cuts made through the A-points or through the D-points are symmetrical with respect to both the longitudinal and transverse axes. When the cuts are made through both points, the resulting laminate is not symmetrical with respect to its longitudinal axis. Although it is a standard laminate, it is not suitable for making a standard third-generation laminate, because there are no midpoints through which cuts can be made. Using these will produce only non-standard laminates. Standard second-generation designs are shown in Photo 13 in chapter 1, the cutting board on the left in Photo 2 (page 17), and Photos 1, 2, 3 (the design in the bottom of the bowl), and 12 (cutting board on the left) in chapter 6.

Photo 3. THE DESIGN ENCIRCLING THIS BOWL IS FROM A THIRD-GENERATION MITERED LAMINATE; 13 X 10¼ INCHES (33 X 26 CM); MAHOGANY, CHERRY, WALNUT, MAPLE, POPLAR, AND TWO UNKNOWN WOOD SPECIES.

Photo 4. CLOCK WITH THIRD-GENERATION DESIGN MADE BY USING THE MITERED LAMINATE PROCESS; 7 X ½ INCH (18 X 1.5 CM); WALNUT, MAPLE, AND CHERRY

Photo 5. CUTTING BOARDS MADE BY USING THE MITERED LAMINATE PROCESS: (LEFT) MADE FROM TWO SECOND-GENERATION DESIGNS, 15 X 11 X 1 INCHES (38 X 28 X 2.5 CM), CHERRY, POPLAR, AND THREE UNKNOWN WOOD SPECIES; (MIDDLE BACK) A FIRST-GENERATION DESIGN, 12 X 10 X 1⅛ INCH (30.5 X 25.5 X 2.8 CM), WALNUT, OAK, TEAK, MAPLE, ELM, BIRCH, CHERRY, NARRA, AVOIDIRE, ROSEWOOD, ASH, AND HICKORY (MADE BY JAMES WALTER RANNEFELD); (RIGHT) A THIRD-GENERATION DESIGN, 13 X 12 X ¾ INCH (33 X 30.5 X 2 CM) IN WALNUT, CHERRY, AND MAPLE

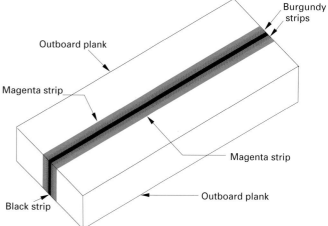

Figure 1. STANDARD LINEAR LAMINATE WITH A STRIPE MADE OF FIVE STRIPS

Standard Third-Generation Laminates

Standard second-generation laminates are converted into standard third-generation laminates by first cutting the mitered laminate at an angle through either the A-points, the D-points, or both. Although it is not usually difficult to determine where the A-points and the D-points are located, a few designs will present a challenge. In some patterns, part of the design stripe is a straight line that coincides with the longitudinal centerline. The A-points and the D-points are located on this centerline, halfway between the other features of the design, where they alternate above and below the centerline. The points also are halfway between the two cut faces of each section.

In viewing the design from left to right, if the feature other than the straight line (which coincides with the centerline) is below the centerline and the next one is above, the midpoint between the two is the A-point. In the opposite situation, going from a higher to a lower feature, or descending, the midpoint is a D-point.

After the cross sections are cut at some constant angle, every other section is turned over. The sections are then glued together, matching the design from one section to the next. As described for second-generation designs, three different third-generation laminates are derived from each second-generation laminate at any angle. Two will be symmetrical with respect to both axes. The other, which results from cutting through both the A-points and the D-points, will not be symmetrical with respect to its longitudinal axis. Though it is a standard design, it cannot be used for making a standard next-generation pattern. Standard third-generation designs are found in Photos 3 and 4 in this chapter (page 19) and Photo 18 in chapter 6.

The entire process can be continued. Symmetrical third-generation laminates can be converted into standard fourth-generation designs in exactly the same manner as described above. These, in turn, can be converted to fifth-generation laminates and so forth. Theoretically, there is no limit to how far this can be carried out. Photo 5 (page 19) shows three standard designs: the upper cutting board is made with a first-generation laminate; the board on the left has two second-generation laminates; the one on the left exhibits a third-generation design.

Standard Designs

There are a large number of designs that can be made following the standard process. Consider using only one cutting angle for making all the conversions. As was stated earlier, a first-generation laminate can be converted into three second-generation laminates. Two out of these three second-generation laminates can each be converted into three third-generation laminates. This results in a total of six third-generation laminates. Of these six, four (two out of each three) can be made into three fourth-generation patterns, for a total of twelve designs. Two-thirds of the latter, or eight, can be converted into 24 different standard fifth-generation laminates. These result from the use of only one cutting angle.

If only two angles are used throughout, then a linear laminate yields two standard first-generation laminates. With two angles, each of these would yield six new designs, for a total of 12 second-generation laminates from two zigzag patterns. A third of these cannot be used for making a standard third-generation laminate. Each of the other eight would produce three new designs at one angle, a total of six with a second angle. The total would be three designs per angle multiplied by two angles, then multiplied by eight second-generation laminates, a total of 48 designs. Conversion to the next generation would result in two-thirds of 48 designs times three designs per angle, multiplied by two angles, for a total of 192 new standard fourth-generation designs.

The calculations above indicate the large change in the number of designs as the number of angles changes or as the laminate is taken to a higher generation. Table 1 illustrates this fact for up to four angles and five generations.

TYPE OF STANDARD MITERED LAMINATE	ONE CUTTING ANGLE	TWO CUTTING ANGLES	THREE CUTTING ANGLES	FOUR CUTTING ANGLES
First Generation	1	2	3	4
Second Generation	3	12	27	48
Third Generation	6	48	162	384
Fourth Generation	12	192	972	3,072
Fifth Generation	24	768	5,832	24,576

Table 1. TOTAL NUMBER OF STANDARD LAMINATES

Chapter 3
Tools and Techniques

While the process of making mitered laminates is simple, the necessary techniques are exact and demanding. A mitered laminate is made up of many small pieces of wood that are mitered at more than one angle, and these wood pieces must fit so perfectly that it is difficult to see the glue lines; this means that all cuts must be made at the proper angle and that all cut surfaces must be flat and smooth. Some of the ways that this can be accomplished are discussed in this chapter. I will share with you the techniques and aids that I have developed to help me achieve excellent joints in mitered designs.

Photo 1. AN ASSORTMENT OF WOOD PIECES THAT CAN BE USED IN THE MITERED LAMINATE PROCESS

Photo 2. CLOCKWISE FROM TOP RIGHT: ELECTRIC BELT SANDER, HAND PLANE, TENON SAW, KEYHOLE SAW, AND SANDING BLOCK WITH SANDPAPER (LOWER LEFT)

Materials and Tools

Before beginning a project, you should determine whether you have the necessary materials and tools to carry out the work. The materials required for making mitered laminates are available to most woodworkers. For a standard laminate, at least two species of wood are needed, preferably woods with contrasting colors. You can use either softwoods or hardwoods, but woods that have a tendency to split, crack, or splinter should be avoided. For most projects, planks ¾ to 1 inch (2 to 2.5 cm) thick are ideal. It is easier to work with softwoods, especially if you have to work with basic hand tools. Using hardwood takes more effort and time, but the finished product can be given a more enduring and beautiful finish. A variety of woods that can be used is pictured in Photo 1.

Hand tools are adequate for those with the necessary skills (Photo 2). When making a mitered laminate, a number of woodworking operations have to be performed. A handsaw can be used to saw all the necessary cuts.

To begin, planks must be ripped into two outboard planks and into one or more strips for the stripe. Sawing, of course, is also necessary to cut a laminate into cross sections. This requires skill, since the sections must have smooth and planar edges that are perpendicular to the side of the laminate. After the cross sections have been glued together, you should trim the sharp, jagged edges; this is also easy to do with a saw.

At several steps in the process, you will need to level and smooth the surfaces of the laminates. This can be done with a woodworking plane. When making a linear laminate, the edges and sides of the ripped planks must be planed smooth, straight, and square. This is assurance that the edges, when glued together, will fit properly, leaving no gaps or cracks. After the cross sections have been glued together into a laminate, the two sides again must be planed smooth and planar. For this operation, it is best to use a plane with a very sharp plane iron. If the laminate is to be used in a project, this will decrease the amount of sanding required.

Gluing is an operation that requires a few basic tools and a glue that is easy to use. A liquid glue, either the white or yellow variety, works well and is readily available at a reasonable price at hardware and building-supply stores. A flexible spatula or a stiff brush is adequate for spreading the glue. C-clamps are all that is needed to firmly hold the glued components of a linear mitered laminate together. For gluing cross sections together, pipe or bar clamps work best. See Photo 3.

Though the basic tools necessary for making planar mitered laminates have been discussed, other tools are needed for most projects that are to be enhanced with a laminate. A tape measure and a bench rule measure distances, and a try square marks and checks angles (Photo 4). Either an awl or a pencil can be used for marking. A brace is useful for drilling holes when used in conjunction with auger bits and twist drills; many woodworkers have access to an electric drill, which performs the same function, only faster (Photo 5).

Sharpening various tools requires a file or an oil stone. A hammer and a screwdriver have many uses. To smooth surfaces for finishing, you will need several grades of sandpaper and a sanding block (see Photo 2). When a lathe is used to complete a project, a set of turning tools is a necessity, but it is helpful to also have a compass and inside and outside calipers (Photo 6). On some projects, it is necessary to use framing or circular clamps (Photo 7).

The labor involved in making mitered laminates can be reduced in several ways. One way is to have more than just the basic tools available. Also, with better and more sophistical tools, it is sometimes possible to increase the quality of the finished product at the same time. Here are two examples in which this is the case: when cutting cross sections, the use of a miter box improves the quality of the cut edges; when smoothing the surface of a laminate, the use of a spoke shave or a cabinet scraper is very effective.

The use of power tools and machinery is usually the most effective way to reduce the labor involved and, in many cases, upgrade the quality of the work at the same time. Portable power tools are available, and most of them can be used to your advantage, although, in some cases, stationary power equipment is even more effective.

Making a Linear Laminate

A linear laminate is composed of a stripe and two outboard planks. The stripe consists of an odd number of thin strips of wood glued together into a long plank. The edges of all components must be smooth, planar, and square. The thin strips should be as wide as the thickness of the outboard planks. Every strip should have a constant width from one end to the other so that the stripe is identical throughout the length. If its thickness varies, the stripe may not match or line up on both sides of the laminate.

All the components should be glued into one unit at the same time. To do this, spread a thin layer of glue over all the matching surfaces. Arrange all the components to be glued in the proper order, with the stripe between the two outboard planks. The edges of the strips should be leveled with the sides or faces of the outboard planks as they are glued together. Do not use excessive pressure in the gluing process as it could squeeze out all the glue and cause the joint to fail.

Improper alignment of the components during the gluing process may cause problems. After the glue has dried, a linear laminate should be planed until both faces are level and smooth. If, in the gluing process, the two outboard planks are slightly offset so that all the faces are in different planes, subsequent planing will usually result in a laminate in which the edges and the stripe are no longer square to the faces of the board. This causes a problem similar to when a stripe width is not constant; when alternate sections are turned over to make a laminate design, the design will not line up on both sides of the laminate.

Photo 3. CLOCKWISE FROM LEFT: CLAMP HOLDER OR CROSS SECTION GLUING JIG WITH PIPE CLAMPS, ASSORTED C-CLAMPS, HAND SCREW, AND SPRING CLAMPS

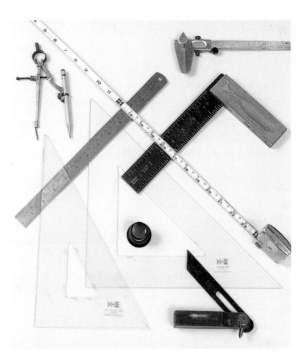

Photo 4. CLOCKWISE FROM THE LOWER LEFT: 30°/60° TRIANGLE, RULER, COMPASS, MEASURING TAPE (CROSSES DIAGONALLY), VERNIER CALIPERS (UPPER RIGHT), TRY SQUARE, ADJUSTABLE BEVEL (LOWER RIGHT), 45°/90° TRIANGLE, AND MAGNIFYING LOOP (CENTER)

Photo 5. CLOCKWISE FROM LEFT: DRILL BIT SET, ELECTRIC DRILL, SPADE BIT, AND DOWEL CENTERS

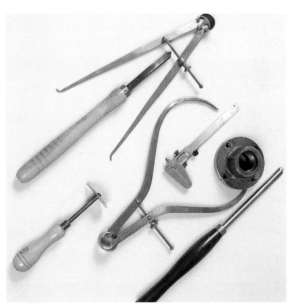

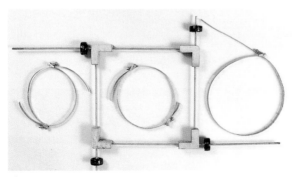

Photo 7. CIRCULAR CLAMPS AND FRAMING CLAMP (CENTER)

Photo 6. CLOCKWISE FROM TOP: INSIDE CALIPERS, OUTSIDE CALIPERS, VERNIER CALIPERS (INSIDE LEGS OF OUTSIDE CALIPERS), LATHE FACE PLATE (GREEN), LATHE BOWL GOUGE, SCRAPER (BOTTOM LEFT), AND LATHE PARTING TOOL (TOP LEFT)

Cutting Cross Sections

A first-generation laminate is made from a linear laminate by cutting the laminate into cross sections then gluing these sections back together in a different manner. Cutting laminates into cross sections is the most demanding step in the entire process. Every cut through the laminate must be made at the same angle. The cuts must be perpendicular to the face of the laminate. In addition, every section must have the same width. The cuts must be smooth and planar so that when sections are glued together they will fit precisely along all cut edges.

Making the cuts described above requires the proper skills and technique. Some woodworkers can make a precise cut using a handsaw. Others may obtain a better result by using a miter box. Still others may prefer to use some type of power tool. I get the most consistent results by using a jig on a table saw called a *sliding table cutoff jig*. It is sketched in Figure 1 along with the necessary attachments for cutting a linear laminate into cross sections. Photo 8 shows the cutoff jig without any attachments and Photo 9 shows most of the attachments needed for cutting the cross sections.

This jig has a plywood base about the same size as the top of the table saw. Underneath, it is equipped with cleats that fit the miter gauge slots on the saw. This allows the jig to slide back and forth across the top of the table saw. A 2 x 6 is screwed onto the top of the plywood base and across its front to provide stability. An adjustable

angle fence is positioned on the left side of the jig. On the right side, near the front of the jig, is an adjustable stop fence A toggle clamp is firmly attached to the table and is used to rigidly hold the laminate in place while miter cuts are being made. See Figure 1.

To use this jig for cutting cross sections from a linear laminate, set the angle fence at the desired cutting angle. Practice making cuts with scrap stock. When you have the correct angle, set the stop fence to the desired width of a cross section. Again, practice cutting scrap stock to achieve the exact width by pushing the laminate against the angle fence and cutting off its end. Then push the laminate firmly against both fences and clamp in place. Push the jig through the saw blade, cutting off a section. If the cross section does not have the correct width, adjust the stop fence accordingly, and repeat the process until the cross sections have the correct width. Repeat the procedure for all additional sections.

Gluing Cross Sections

If these sections are arranged correctly, placed side by side, then glued together in the prescribed manner, a standard first-generation mitered laminate is produced. This type of laminate always has a zigzag pattern; a steep pattern results when a small cutting angle is used and, as the cutting angle becomes larger, the pattern gradually becomes flatter.

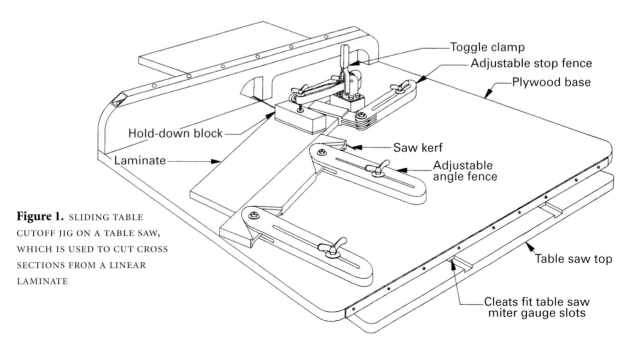

Figure 1. SLIDING TABLE CUTOFF JIG ON A TABLE SAW, WHICH IS USED TO CUT CROSS SECTIONS FROM A LINEAR LAMINATE

Toggle clamp
Adjustable stop fence
Plywood base
Hold-down block
Saw kerf
Laminate
Adjustable angle fence
Table saw top
Cleats fit table saw miter gauge slots

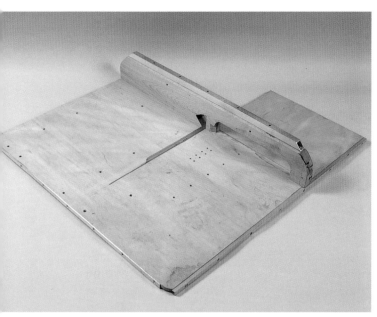

Photo 8. SLIDING TABLE CUTOFF JIG SHOWN WITHOUT ANY ATTACHMENTS

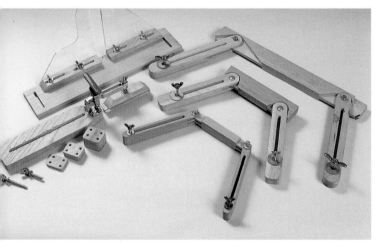

Photo 9. ATTACHMENTS FOR JIG, CLOCKWISE FROM TOP RIGHT: ANGLE FENCE, STOP FENCES, ELEVATION BLOCKS FOR TOGGLE CLAMPS, SCREWS FOR FENCE (BOTTOM, FAR LEFT), TOGGLE CLAMP, AND SCRIBED-LINE POSITIONING JIG

To obtain this pattern, alternate cross sections should be turned end over end or edge over edge. Turning a section once causes the stripe that ran from the lower left to the upper right to run from the upper left to the lower right, or vice versa. Before gluing, the cross sections are all assembled in this fashion, with the cut edges positioned facing each other.

The stripe at the edge of the cut on one cross section must exactly match or line up with the stripe in the adjoining section. Before actually gluing these together, check every joint to be sure that the stripe matches up properly. Generally more precise matchups are obtained if the cross sections are reglued in the same order in which they were cut from the laminate. I usually number the cross sections consecutively as I cut them off, and, if they match up in this order, I glue them back that way. (In some of the photos in this book, a few of these numbers are still visible.) These markings will be sanded off later.

Matching up a single-stripe laminate is usually very easy. With a very complex stripe, however, and especially with a mitered laminate in which each cut was made through more than one element of the design, it becomes more difficult. Then it may be necessary to try more than one cross section before a match is found. This is an indication that the accuracy of the cutting operation is not as good as it should be. If you have problems finding accurate design matches, your cutting accuracy probably needs to be improved.

I have gotten satisfactory results with the following gluing procedure. Apply glue to one joint at a time by placing a thin bead of glue along the cut edge of a cross section. Place this section in contact with the mating edge of the mating section and rub the two together until the glue has been spread over the entire mating area of the two sections. Repeat the procedure by running a bead of glue along the other edge of one of these sections, and repeat this glue spreading technique, using the third cross section. Repeat, using a fourth cross section, thus spreading glue over three joints. Clamp these sections firmly together, having matched up the stripe at each joint.

A small magnifying glass is useful for checking precise matchup (see Photo 4). If a joint is not matched up correctly, loosen the clamp, correct the mismatch, and reclamp. When all the joints are perfectly matched up, reclamp the sections for about five minutes. The joints will then have bonded sufficiently, and the assembly can be unclamped so that additional sections can be glued on. To do this, spread a bead of glue on the edge of an end cross section, and repeat the above procedure, each time applying glue to three more joints before the assembly is reclamped. When all the cross sections have been glued together in this manner, leave the assembly clamped for about six hours. Do not use excessive pressure as the cross sections can become misaligned.

An ordinary pipe or bar clamp works best for clamping all types of cross sections. For short sections, one clamp is needed, but when the cross sections are long, two should be used. To equalize the pressure along the length of the cross sections during the gluing process, use a stiff board or block (that is as long as the cross sections) between each of the two end sections and the faces of the clamp.

To facilitate the gluing process, I made a simple clamp holder or cradle from wood. For a single clamp, use two 3-inch-wide (7.5 cm) boards that are somewhat thicker than the height of the pipe or bar clamp and about 24 inches (61 cm) long. Place these side by side with a space in between wide enough for the bar or pipe. Nail a plywood cross member near each end of the planks to hold the two planks in place. Then place the clamp in this slot. Nail a stiff board or block at a right angle to the two boards and in front of the clamp face at the end of the clamp where the tightening screw is located. Use a similar board or block at the other end of the clamp but do not nail it on. These boards or blocks bear against the end cross sections when they are being clamped together. The clamp holder in Photo 3 (left) shows a clamp holder made to hold two clamps.

After the glue has dried, the laminate should be trimmed. The sharp ends that were on the cross sections are now on the two edges of the laminate. Trim these off, leaving edges that are straight and even. The cuts should be parallel to the design and to each other. In addition, these edges should be square with the ends of the laminate. Then sand the mitered laminate until each face is smooth, planar, and parallel to the other face. It can be used in this fashion for a project, or it can be converted to the next generation laminate.

Cutting a Generation Laminate

Cutting standard cross sections from a mitered laminate requires a different technique than cutting sections from a linear laminate. It is no longer an option to cut the cross sections to any width. The laminate must be cut at specific points along its length. Cuts at other points result in a nonstandard laminate and produce laminates in which the design in one section will not line up with the design in an adjoining cross section.

Cuts must be made through the exact centers of either the ascending (up) legs, the descending (down) legs, or both legs of the design. The term *leg* refers to the center strip of the stripe that goes across every cross section from one edge to the other, either in a straight or an angled line. It crosses the longitudinal centerline of each cross section. In most standard laminates, the legs go from the lower left edge to the upper right edge in one cross section and in the opposite direction in the two adjoining sections. The stripe alternates in this fashion unless it goes straight across every section.

It is not wise to try to cut these sections to specific widths as you did the linear laminate. A slight error in width quickly multiplies into a large error as the number of cut sections increases. When making these cuts, it is difficult to judge by eye where the exact center of the leg is.

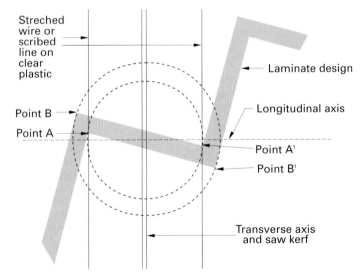

Figure 2. HOW A DESIGN IS CENTERED WITH STRETCHED WIRES OR SCRIBED LINES ON PLASTIC, SHOWN WITH STRETCHED WIRES OR SCRIBED LINES GOING THROUGH THE A-POINTS

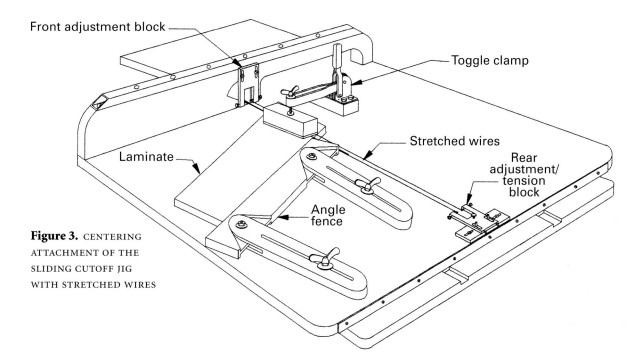

Front adjustment block

Toggle clamp

Laminate

Stretched wires

Rear adjustment/ tension block

Angle fence

Figure 3. CENTERING
ATTACHMENT OF THE
SLIDING CUTOFF JIG
WITH STRETCHED WIRES

However, the points at the mitered junctions where the design changes direction can be accurately pinpointed. There are pairs of such points, called *corresponding points*, which are an equal distance from the exact center of the design. These are points that can be used as guides to find the center points. Figure 2 shows two pairs of corresponding points in a design: points A and A' and points B and B'. The circles in the figure show that each pair is an equal distance from the central point.

I made two versions of an attachment that fits on the sliding table cutoff jig. These attachments help to cut a laminate design through its center points, using the corresponding points as a means of accurately positioning the laminate. One jig uses two stretched wires as shown in Figure 3. It is called the *stretched-wire attachment.* The wires run from the front to the rear of the sliding jig.

The wires extend on either side of the saw blade and must be properly positioned to be accurate in cutting the laminate into two equal parts. The adjustment blocks on both ends of the wires can be moved up and down and right and left. The wires must be just high enough to permit the laminate to slide underneath. They must

be parallel to each other, parallel to the plane of the saw blade, and equal in distance from the saw blade, one on the left and one on the right. The distance between the wires must be the same as the distance between the corresponding points on the design as discussed above. The wires must be stretched tightly.

After the wires have been accurately adjusted, push the mitered laminate against the angle fence. (The stop fence is not required and is removed.) Position it so that a pair of corresponding points is located directly below the two wires. Clamp the laminate in place and cut off its end.

The cutoff end is used to check the accuracy of the cut. This end is turned end over end and its cut edge positioned against the cut edge of the laminate. For an acceptable cut, the design must line up at the joint, and the design on one side of the joint must be a mirror image of the design on the other side. If either is not the case, the cut has not been made directly through the center point. The wires must be repositioned accordingly and retested by making more trial cuts until it meets these criteria. Once accurately adjusted, continue the cutting operation until all the cross sections have been cut.

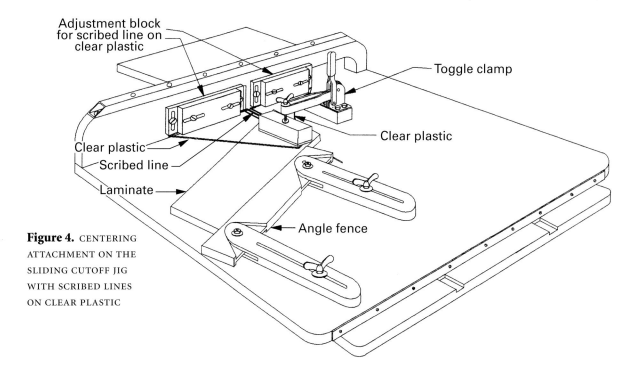

Figure 4. CENTERING
ATTACHMENT ON THE
SLIDING CUTOFF JIG
WITH SCRIBED LINES
ON CLEAR PLASTIC

Another type of attachment, the *scribed-line attachment*, accomplishes the same purpose and is shown in Figure 4. Two adjustable blocks are attached to the 2 x 6 board that stabilizes the front of the sliding table. One is located on the left and the other on the right of the saw blade. These blocks can be moved up and down and right and left. A triangular piece of clear plastic is attached underneath each block, parallel to the top of the sliding jig with one edge parallel to the plane of the saw blade. A fine line is drawn on the underside of each plastic piece near the edge that is parallel to the saw blade. These lines are adjusted and positioned as were the wires above. When making a cut, the scribed lines should be positioned directly above a pair of corresponding points on the pattern. Using the procedure described for the other attachment, test the accuracy of the cut, then cut the remainder of the laminate into sections.

The scribed-line attachment was slightly modified to simplify the process of positioning the attachment. Photo 9 (page 25) shows the modified scribed-line attachment (upper left) along with the other attachments used on the sliding jig. In this version, the two up-and-down blocks have been combined in one block. The edge of each clear plastic triangle (instead of the scribed line) is used as the guide in positioning. Each edge is cut with the saw blade so it is perfectly parallel to it.

Then a shim of the proper width (determined by trial and error) is used between the saw blade and the edges of the plastic triangles so that the two edges are an equal distance from the saw blade and, at the same time, as far apart as the two corresponding parts. These edges are then positioned directly over the corresponding points. This modification greatly simplifies the process of adjusting the guides and decreases the time required. (I still call it the scribed-line attachment and prefer it over the stretched-wire model.) I have devised a simple tool for retrieving sections from under the scribed-line jig attachment. It is made of bent wire, as shown in Photo 10.

Either attachment can be readily made in the shop. Each requires materials that are readily available—either in your shop or from a hardware or building-supply store. These stores also sell the clear plastic, which is normally used in place of glass for glazing windows or doors.

The same procedure is used for gluing these cross sections together as was described for those cut from the linear laminate. The same procedure is also followed for trueing and squaring the edges and leveling the faces of the mitered laminate. This can then be used to enhance

Photo 10. A HANDMADE TOOL USED TO RETRIEVE SECTIONS FROM UNDERNEATH THE SCRIBED-LINE JIG ATTACHMENT AFTER CROSS SECTIONS ARE CUT

Photo 11. A VARIETY OF CROSS SECTIONS, COMBINED ITEMS, AND MISCELLANEOUS PIECES OF WOODEN ITEMS LEFT OVER FROM DIFFERENT PROJECTS

a project or convert to a next-generation laminate. Subsequent conversions are carried out in the same manner as described above.

A mitered laminate can't be treated as a board or plank in shop operations. The laminate cannot be planed, joined, or shaped on mechanized equipment. The knives split out small pieces of wood, leaving a rough surface. This happens because the wood grain runs in many directions in every laminate, and the glue joints are not as strong as is normally the case, since you are, in many cases, gluing end grain to end grain. The glued joints are, however, adequate for most other shop operations. A mitered laminate can be turned on a lathe (when the tools are sharp). Other shaping operations, such as sawing, routing, and sanding, also work well with mitered laminates. Sanding is the preferred method for leveling and smoothing the mitered laminate faces. Using a belt sander speeds up this process (see Photo 2 on page 21).

In making any project, various pieces of wood (leftover or cutoff pieces) are created but never used. Photos 11 and 12 show some of these pieces.

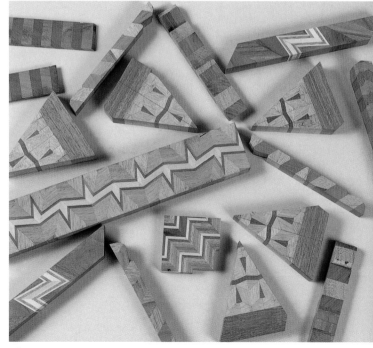

Photo 12. A NUMBER OF DIFFERENT CROSS SECTIONS, SECTORS, SEGMENTS, GLUED-UP STRUCTURES, AND SO FORTH THAT WERE NOT USED IN PROJECTS

Chapter 4
Standard Laminate Designs

This chapter will explain and illustrate the mitered laminate process from another viewpoint, with illustrations showing the processes and designs for the three first-generation, the 27 second-generation, and the 162 third-generation designs that result when every combination of cuts (at three different angles) is made. In addition, the chapter discusses how any of these standard laminates can be further enhanced if the outboard planks used in making the linear laminate have a distinct, straight wood grain.

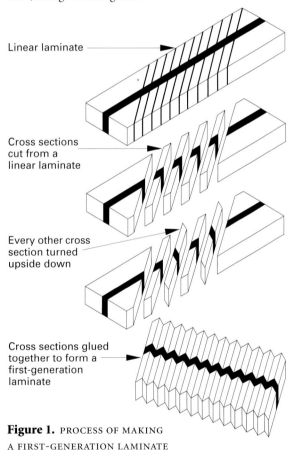

Linear laminate

Cross sections cut from a linear laminate

Every other cross section turned upside down

Cross sections glued together to form a first-generation laminate

Figure 1. PROCESS OF MAKING A FIRST-GENERATION LAMINATE

Standard Mitered Laminate Designs Visualized

Though the laminating process was described in the previous chapter, it may be difficult to visualize the steps involved. Figures 1, 2, and 3 depict the process of going from a linear laminate with a single dark stripe to a third-generation mitered laminate.

Figure 1 shows a standard linear laminate cut into four cross sections of equal width. (The cross sections were cut at the heavier diagonal lines.) The second and fourth sections from the left are then turned upside down and glued together, with the stripe in one section matching the stripe in each of the adjoining sections. As you can see, the stripe now forms a zigzag pattern. This is a standard first-generation mitered laminate.

Figure 2 illustrates the steps involved in making the next-generation laminate. This process begins with the first-generation laminate. The first-generation laminate is cut into cross sections (the cuts, shown as heavier diagonal lines, are made through the center points of the descending legs or D-points of the zigzag pattern). Then every other cross section is turned upside down. The illustration at the bottom of this figure shows these sections glued together, with the stripe where the cross sections join lined up. Thus, a standard second-generation is formed.

The second-generation laminate in Figure 2 can then be converted into a third-generation laminate, as shown in Figure 3. The second-generation laminate is cut through the D-points (shown as heavier diagonal lines) into cross sections of equal width. Then, alternate cross sections are turned upside down. The stripe is matched, going from one section to the next; these sections are glued together, and the result is a new laminate with a different design—a standard third-generation design.

A fourth-generation laminate can be made from this third-generation laminate by following the same procedure, the fourth-generation laminate can be converted to a fifth-generation laminate, and the process can be repeated as often as desired, with each conversion producing a new design.

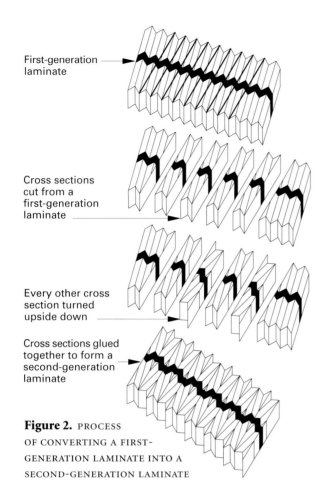

First-generation laminate

Cross sections cut from a first-generation laminate

Every other cross section turned upside down

Cross sections glued together to form a second-generation laminate

Figure 2. PROCESS OF CONVERTING A FIRST-GENERATION LAMINATE INTO A SECOND-GENERATION LAMINATE

Three Generations of Mitered Laminate Designs

A different design is created when the cutting angle at any stage is changed or if the other legs or both legs are cut. To show the wide variety of standard designs possible, all patterns in the first three generations, using all combinations of only three angles (30°, 45°, and 60°) are shown in Figures 4 through Figure 60 (see page 33 and following).

In each figure, the entire process of converting a linear laminate into a first-generation, a second-generation, and three third-generation laminates is shown. The design is indicated as a heavy magenta line. The previously cut faces of the cross sections (or glue lines) are shown as light black lines. The heavier diagonal lines in each illustration are the points and angles at which the laminates are cut. These cuts produce the cross sections for the next generation laminate. The arrows show the direction of the change in the process from one generation to the next.

The process starts with a linear laminate at the upper left corner of each figure. Just below this is the first-generation laminate that is formed by gluing the cross sections together (using the standard procedure). To the right of this (in the center of the figure) is the

Figure 3. PROCESS OF CONVERTING A SECOND-GENERATION LAMINATE INTO A THIRD-GENERATION LAMINATE

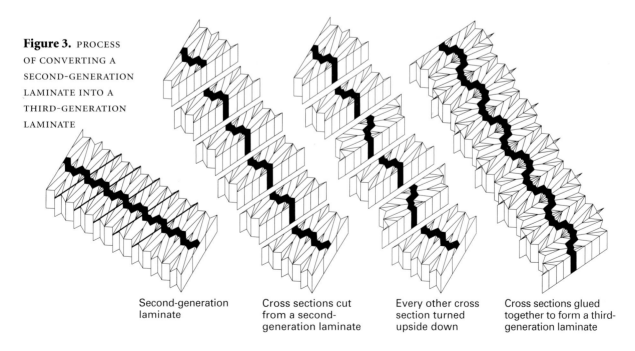

Second-generation laminate

Cross sections cut from a second-generation laminate

Every other cross section turned upside down

Cross sections glued together to form a third-generation laminate

second-generation laminate that results from gluing together the sections cut from the first-generation laminate at the places and angles shown. On the right side of each figure are the three third-generation laminates that result from gluing together the cross sections cut from the second-generation laminate. The results of cutting through A-points, D-points, and both are shown, and a design number is given under the patterns for identification. (What the letters and numbers under each drawing mean is explained in chapter 7.)

Though there are actually 27 second-generation designs possible, using combinations of three angles only, only 18 of these are included in the first 57 figures. These 18 are symmetrical with respect to their longitudinal axes and can be converted to the next generation of standard laminates. The other nine are not symmetrical and cannot be converted to standard mitered laminates. The latter were made by cutting the first-generation laminates through both the A-points and D-points and gluing these sections together. Figures 58, 59, and 60 illustrate the process used to make each of these nine laminates.

As shown in Table 1 in chapter 2 (page 20) and in the drawings in Figures 4 through 60, there are a total of 192 standard designs in the first three generations, using only three cutting angles. The designs in these drawings were not all drawn to the same scale, since the width of different cross sections varies widely. These illustrations represent only a small fraction of the many designs and patterns possible. Chapter 5 will discuss how a small change in one or more of the variables in the process affects the final design. These designs are further enhanced if you begin the process with a more complex stripe, especially one with several different species and colors of wood.

All mitered laminates, including the standard ones illustrated above, can be further enhanced if the outboard planks used for making the linear laminate have a distinct grain pattern. In Figures 61, 62, 63, and 64, wood grain has been simulated by narrowly spaced, wavy lines. The heavier black lines represent glue joints, the line where two cross sections are joined. All the glue lines are shown in each illustration. The angled dotted lines represent the cutting angle and location; the stripe is represented by a wide black line. Figure 61 represents the linear laminate.

In the first-generation laminate (Figure 62), the wood grain runs in a zigzag fashion in the same direction as the stripe. Converting this into a second-generation laminate (Figure 63) produces subtle zigzag wood grain designs in addition to the regular pattern made by the stripe. Each zigzag design is made up of mitered blocks of wood in which all the grain runs in the same direction. Although the grain runs in one direction in one pattern, it runs in a different direction in the designs just above and below it. This pattern is converted to two different ones when the second-generation laminate is converted into the next generation (Figure 64).

Note that when making laminates from wood that has a straight and distinct grain, the patterns discussed above are generally easier to see in a laminate than they are in the illustrations. It is the second-generation laminates that exhibit the zigzag grain designs in which the grain runs in one direction in any one pattern and in another direction in the adjacent patterns. Third-generation and higher mitered laminates exhibit a large variety of different and interesting grain patterns. The illustrations in this chapter represent only one example of the many designs possible.

Figure 4

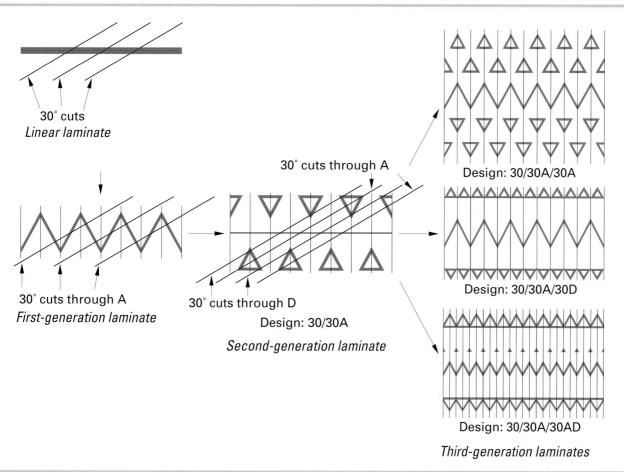

30° cuts
Linear laminate

30° cuts through A
First-generation laminate

30° cuts through A

30° cuts through D
Design: 30/30A

Second-generation laminate

Design: 30/30A/30A

Design: 30/30A/30D

Design: 30/30A/30AD

Third-generation laminates

Figure 5

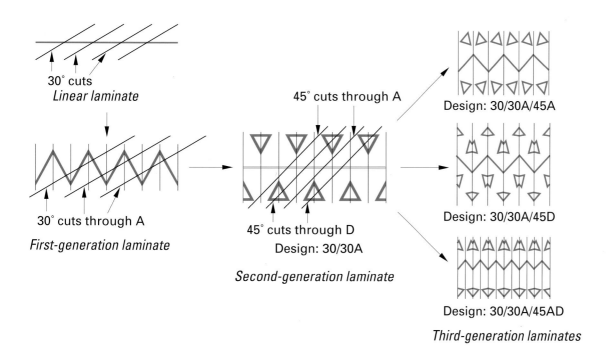

30° cuts
Linear laminate

30° cuts through A
First-generation laminate

45° cuts through A

45° cuts through D
Design: 30/30A

Second-generation laminate

Design: 30/30A/45A

Design: 30/30A/45D

Design: 30/30A/45AD

Third-generation laminates

Figure 6

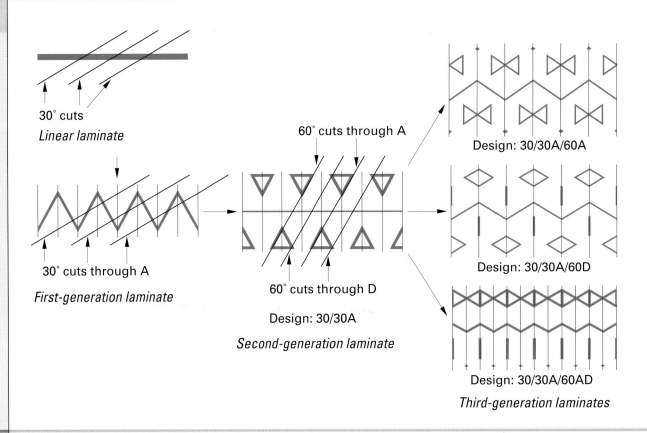

30° cuts
Linear laminate

60° cuts through A

Design: 30/30A/60A

30° cuts through A

First-generation laminate

60° cuts through D

Design: 30/30A

Second-generation laminate

Design: 30/30A/60D

Design: 30/30A/60AD

Third-generation laminates

Figure 7

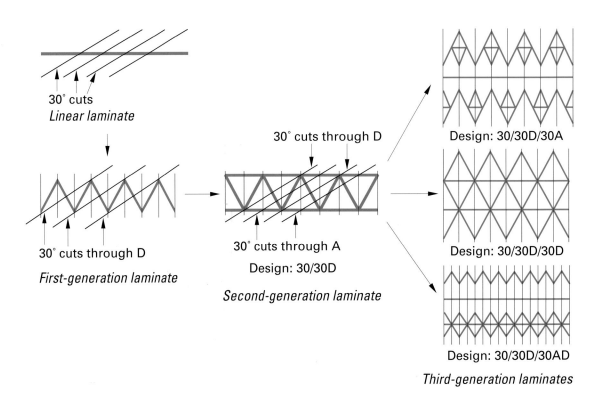

30° cuts
Linear laminate

30° cuts through D

Design: 30/30D/30A

30° cuts through D

First-generation laminate

30° cuts through A

Design: 30/30D

Second-generation laminate

Design: 30/30D/30D

Design: 30/30D/30AD

Third-generation laminates

Figure 8

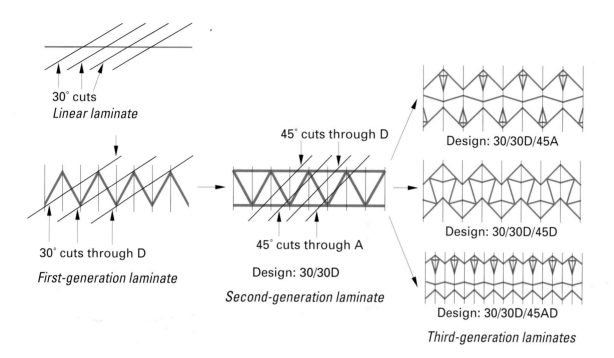

Figure 9

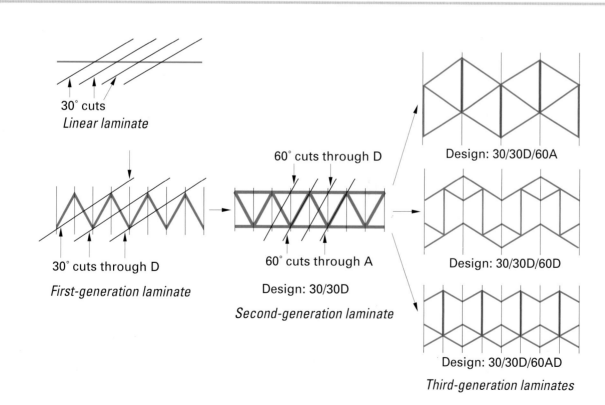

Figure 10

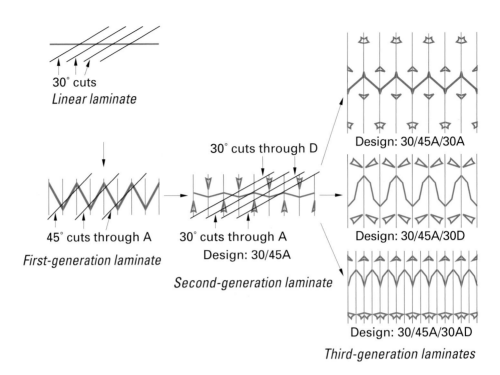

Figure 11

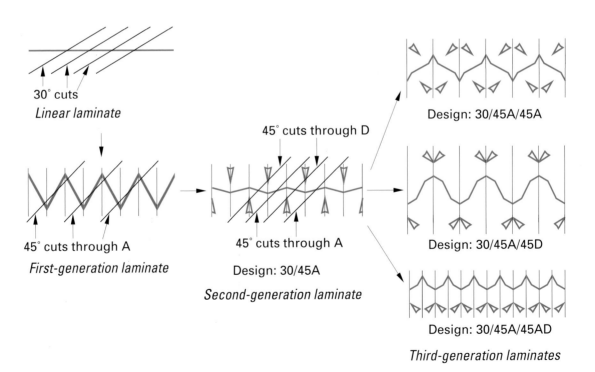

Figure 12

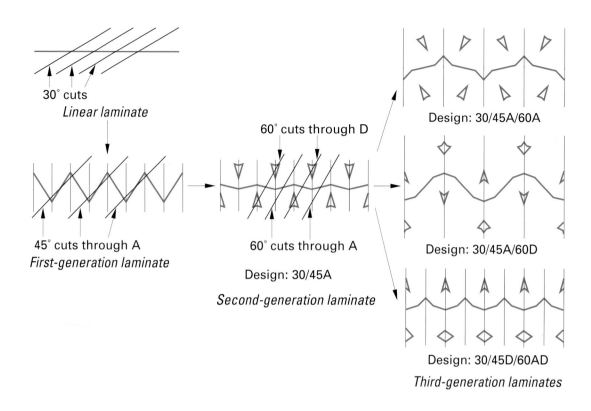

30° cuts
Linear laminate

60° cuts through D

45° cuts through A
First-generation laminate

60° cuts through A

Design: 30/45A
Second-generation laminate

Design: 30/45A/60A

Design: 30/45A/60D

Design: 30/45D/60AD
Third-generation laminates

Figure 13

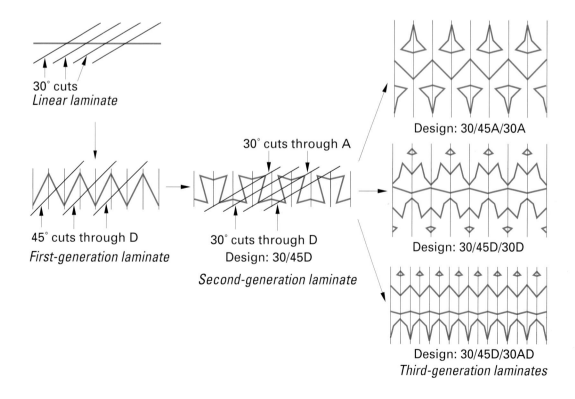

30° cuts
Linear laminate

30° cuts through A

45° cuts through D
First-generation laminate

30° cuts through D
Design: 30/45D
Second-generation laminate

Design: 30/45A/30A

Design: 30/45D/30D

Design: 30/45D/30AD
Third-generation laminates

Figure 14

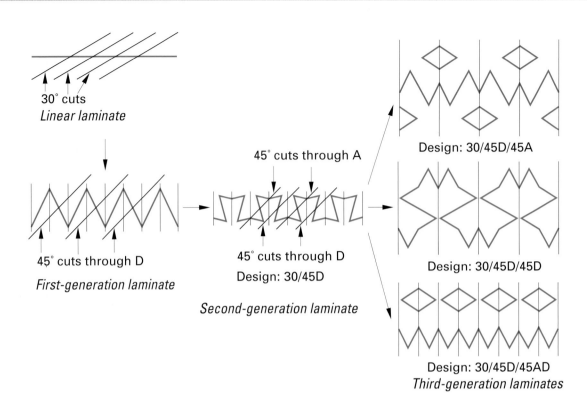

30° cuts
Linear laminate

45° cuts through D
First-generation laminate

45° cuts through A

45° cuts through D
Design: 30/45D

Second-generation laminate

Design: 30/45D/45A

Design: 30/45D/45D

Design: 30/45D/45AD
Third-generation laminates

Figure 15

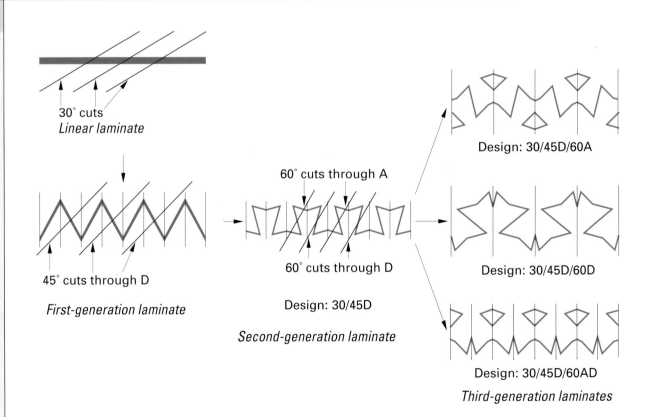

30° cuts
Linear laminate

45° cuts through D
First-generation laminate

60° cuts through A

60° cuts through D
Design: 30/45D

Second-generation laminate

Design: 30/45D/60A

Design: 30/45D/60D

Design: 30/45D/60AD
Third-generation laminates

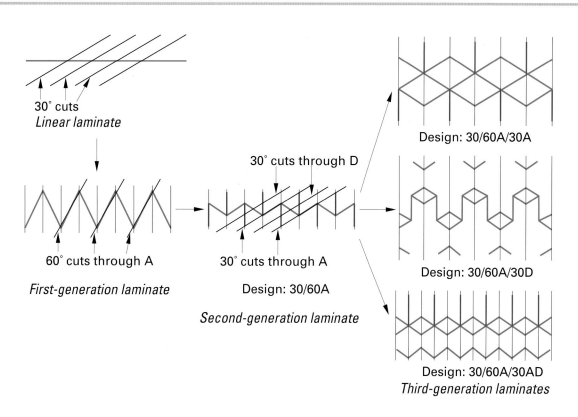

30° cuts
Linear laminate

60° cuts through A

First-generation laminate

30° cuts through D

30° cuts through A

Design: 30/60A

Second-generation laminate

Design: 30/60A/30A

Design: 30/60A/30D

Design: 30/60A/30AD
Third-generation laminates

Figure 17

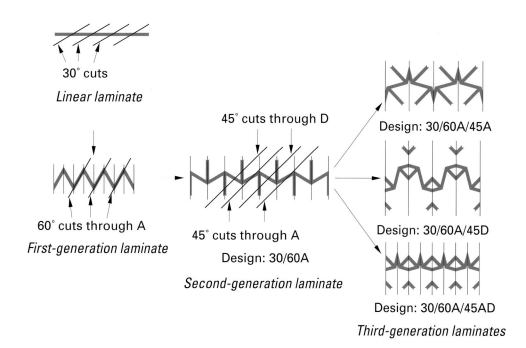

30° cuts
Linear laminate

60° cuts through A
First-generation laminate

45° cuts through D

45° cuts through A

Design: 30/60A

Second-generation laminate

Design: 30/60A/45A

Design: 30/60A/45D

Design: 30/60A/45AD

Third-generation laminates

Figure 18

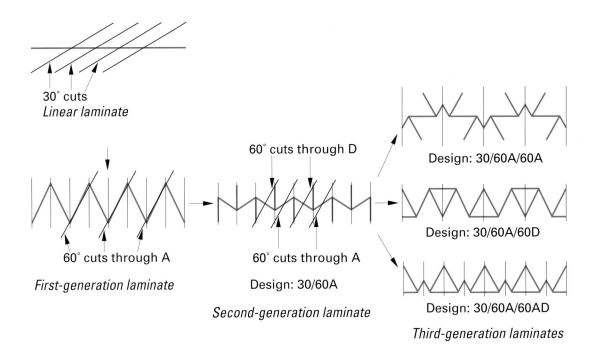

30° cuts
Linear laminate

60° cuts through D

60° cuts through A

60° cuts through A

First-generation laminate

Design: 30/60A

Design: 30/60A/60A

Design: 30/60A/60D

Design: 30/60A/60AD

Second-generation laminate

Third-generation laminates

Figure 19

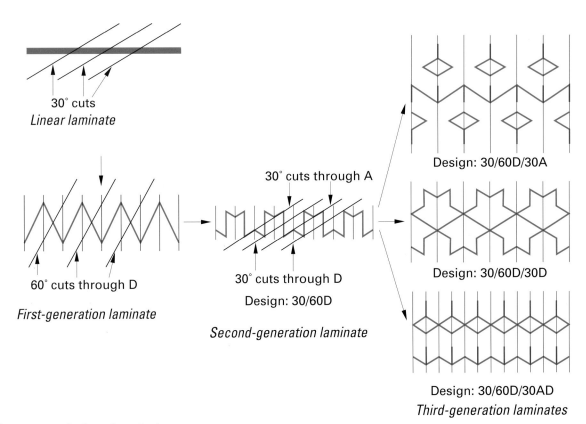

30° cuts
Linear laminate

30° cuts through A

60° cuts through D

30° cuts through D

Design: 30/60D

First-generation laminate

Second-generation laminate

Design: 30/60D/30A

Design: 30/60D/30D

Design: 30/60D/30AD

Third-generation laminates

Figure 20

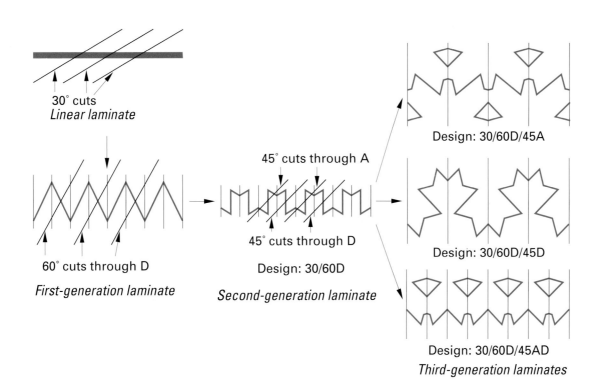

30° cuts
Linear laminate

60° cuts through D

First-generation laminate

45° cuts through A

45° cuts through D

Design: 30/60D

Second-generation laminate

Design: 30/60D/45A

Design: 30/60D/45D

Design: 30/60D/45AD

Third-generation laminates

Figure 21

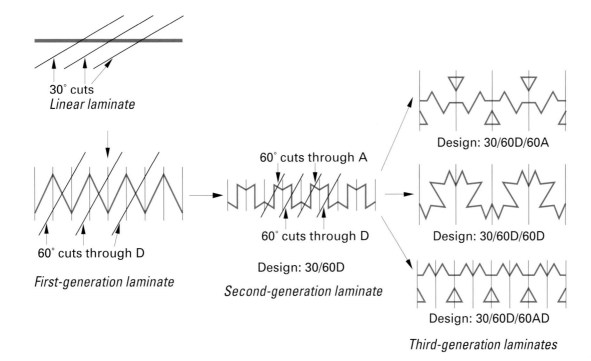

30° cuts
Linear laminate

60° cuts through D

First-generation laminate

60° cuts through A

60° cuts through D

Design: 30/60D

Second-generation laminate

Design: 30/60D/60A

Design: 30/60D/60D

Design: 30/60D/60AD

Third-generation laminates

Figure 22

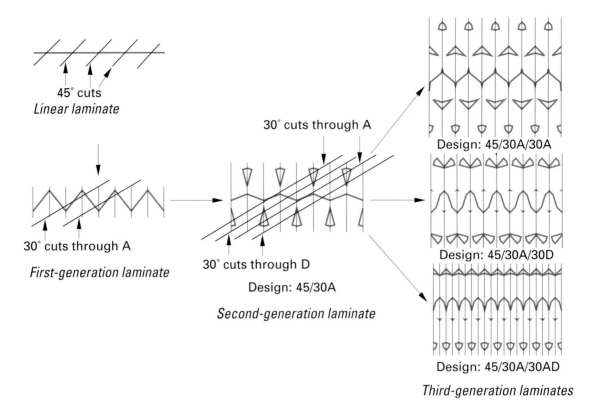

45° cuts
Linear laminate

30° cuts through A
First-generation laminate

30° cuts through A

30° cuts through D

Design: 45/30A

Second-generation laminate

Design: 45/30A/30A

Design: 45/30A/30D

Design: 45/30A/30AD

Third-generation laminates

Figure 23

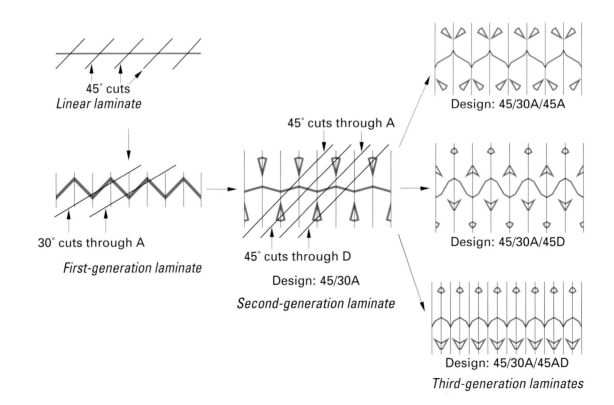

45° cuts
Linear laminate

30° cuts through A
First-generation laminate

45° cuts through A

45° cuts through D

Design: 45/30A

Second-generation laminate

Design: 45/30A/45A

Design: 45/30A/45D

Design: 45/30A/45AD

Third-generation laminates

Figure 24

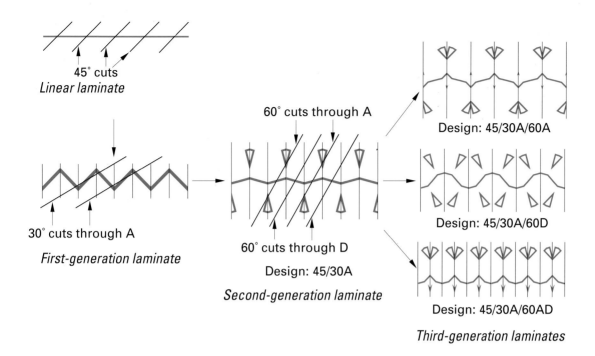

45° cuts
Linear laminate

60° cuts through A

30° cuts through A

First-generation laminate

60° cuts through D

Design: 45/30A

Second-generation laminate

Design: 45/30A/60A

Design: 45/30A/60D

Design: 45/30A/60AD

Third-generation laminates

Figure 25

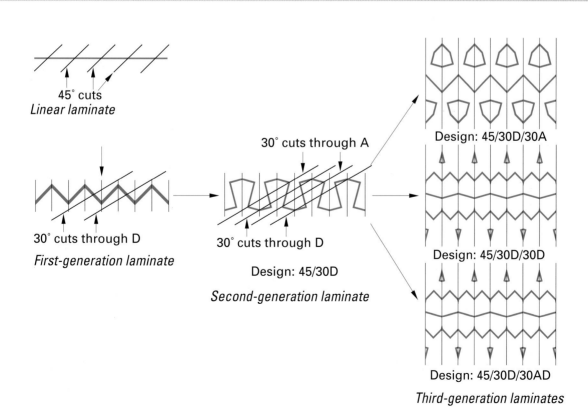

45° cuts
Linear laminate

30° cuts through A

30° cuts through D

First-generation laminate

30° cuts through D

Design: 45/30D

Second-generation laminate

Design: 45/30D/30A

Design: 45/30D/30D

Design: 45/30D/30AD

Third-generation laminates

Figure 26

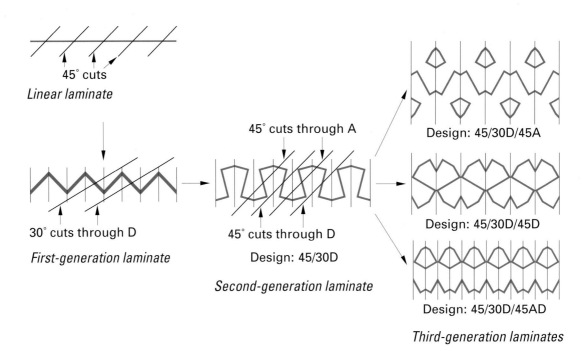

45° cuts
Linear laminate

30° cuts through D

First-generation laminate

45° cuts through A

45° cuts through D

Design: 45/30D

Second-generation laminate

Design: 45/30D/45A

Design: 45/30D/45D

Design: 45/30D/45AD

Third-generation laminates

Figure 27

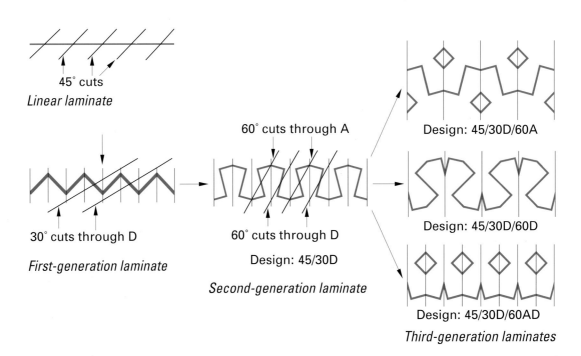

45° cuts
Linear laminate

30° cuts through D

First-generation laminate

60° cuts through A

60° cuts through D

Design: 45/30D

Second-generation laminate

Design: 45/30D/60A

Design: 45/30D/60D

Design: 45/30D/60AD

Third-generation laminates

Figure 28

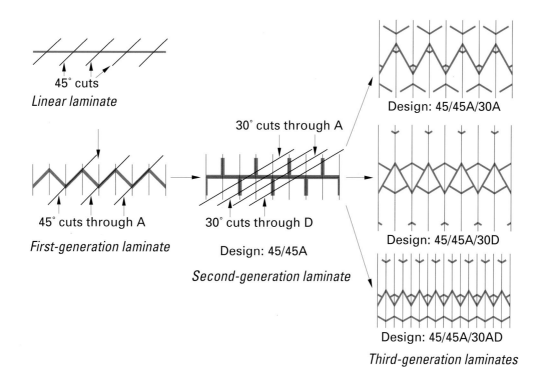

45° cuts
Linear laminate

45° cuts through A
First-generation laminate

30° cuts through A

30° cuts through D

Design: 45/45A
Second-generation laminate

Design: 45/45A/30A

Design: 45/45A/30D

Design: 45/45A/30AD
Third-generation laminates

Figure 29

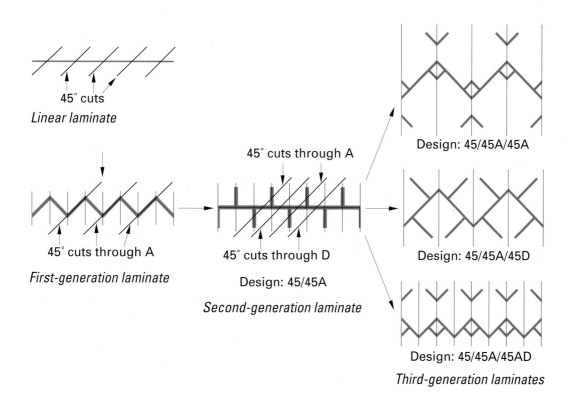

45° cuts
Linear laminate

45° cuts through A
First-generation laminate

45° cuts through A

45° cuts through D

Design: 45/45A
Second-generation laminate

Design: 45/45A/45A

Design: 45/45A/45D

Design: 45/45A/45AD
Third-generation laminates

Figure 30

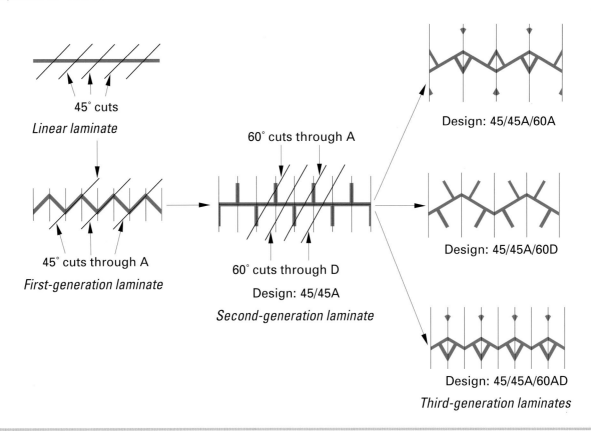

45° cuts

Linear laminate

45° cuts through A

First-generation laminate

60° cuts through A

60° cuts through D

Design: 45/45A

Second-generation laminate

Design: 45/45A/60A

Design: 45/45A/60D

Design: 45/45A/60AD

Third-generation laminates

Figure 31

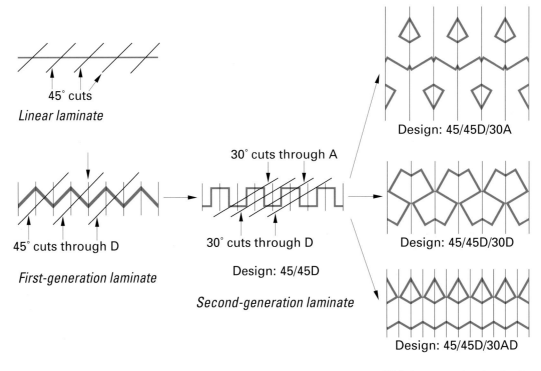

45° cuts

Linear laminate

45° cuts through D

First-generation laminate

30° cuts through A

30° cuts through D

Design: 45/45D

Second-generation laminate

Design: 45/45D/30A

Design: 45/45D/30D

Design: 45/45D/30AD

Third-generation laminates

Figure 32

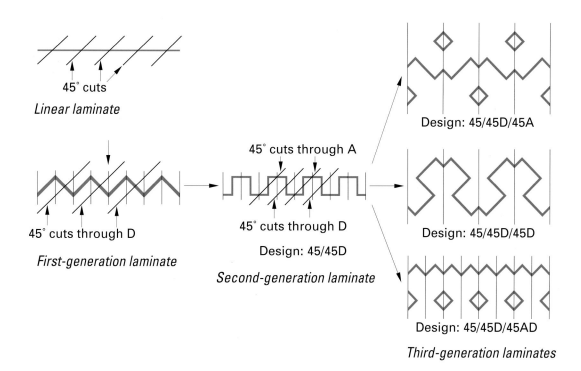

Figure 33

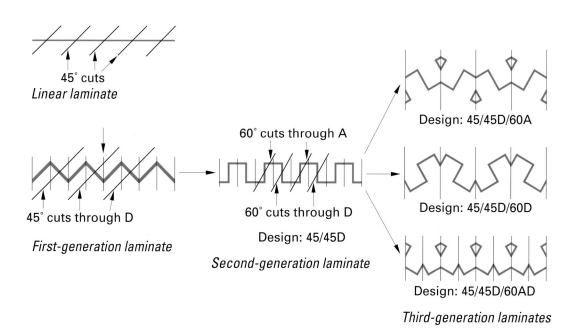

Figure 34

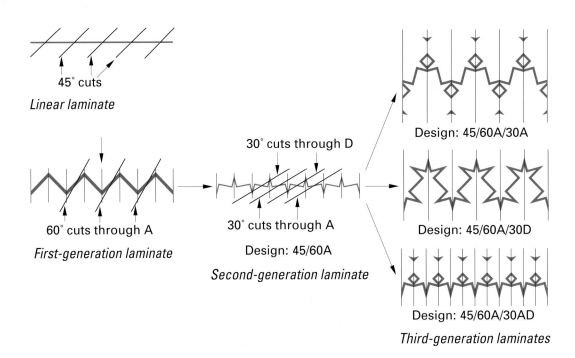

45° cuts

Linear laminate

60° cuts through A

First-generation laminate

30° cuts through D

30° cuts through A

Design: 45/60A

Second-generation laminate

Design: 45/60A/30A

Design: 45/60A/30D

Design: 45/60A/30AD

Third-generation laminates

Figure 35

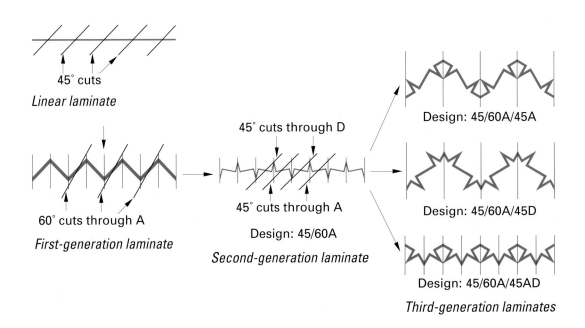

45° cuts

Linear laminate

60° cuts through A

First-generation laminate

45° cuts through D

45° cuts through A

Design: 45/60A

Second-generation laminate

Design: 45/60A/45A

Design: 45/60A/45D

Design: 45/60A/45AD

Third-generation laminates

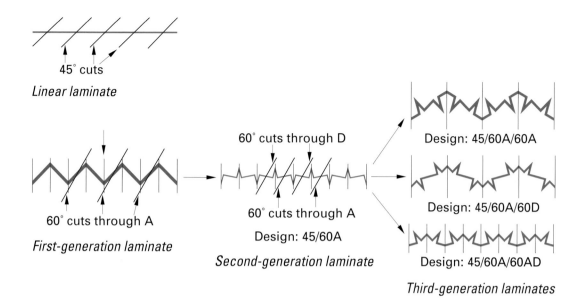

Figure 37

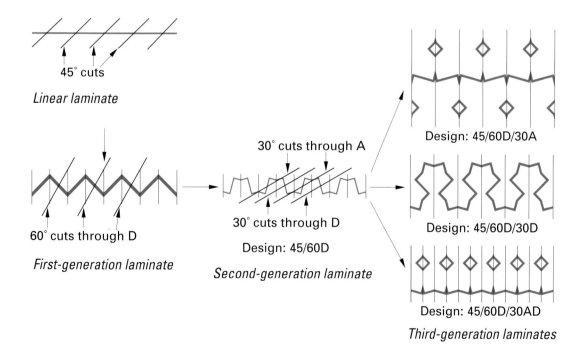

Figure 38

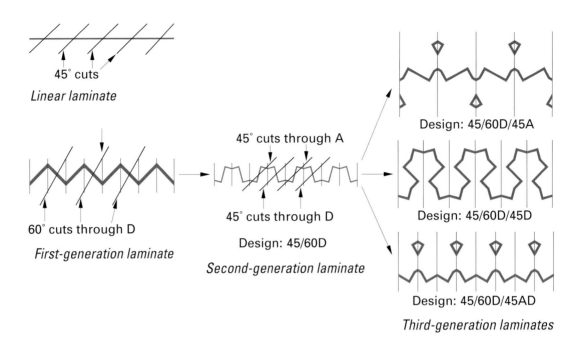

45° cuts
Linear laminate

60° cuts through D
First-generation laminate

45° cuts through A

45° cuts through D

Design: 45/60D
Second-generation laminate

Design: 45/60D/45A

Design: 45/60D/45D

Design: 45/60D/45AD

Third-generation laminates

Figure 39

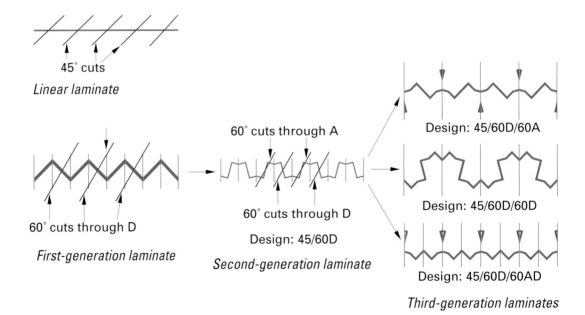

45° cuts
Linear laminate

60° cuts through D
First-generation laminate

60° cuts through A

60° cuts through D

Design: 45/60D
Second-generation laminate

Design: 45/60D/60A

Design: 45/60D/60D

Design: 45/60D/60AD

Third-generation laminates

Figure 40

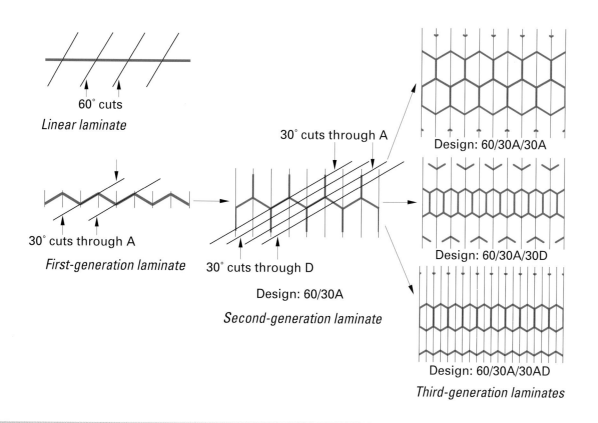

60° cuts

Linear laminate

30° cuts through A

30° cuts through A

First-generation laminate

30° cuts through D

Design: 60/30A

Second-generation laminate

Design: 60/30A/30A

Design: 60/30A/30D

Design: 60/30A/30AD

Third-generation laminates

Figure 41

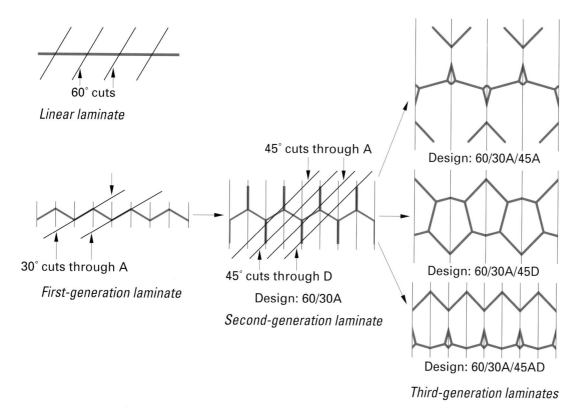

60° cuts

Linear laminate

45° cuts through A

30° cuts through A

First-generation laminate

45° cuts through D

Design: 60/30A

Second-generation laminate

Design: 60/30A/45A

Design: 60/30A/45D

Design: 60/30A/45AD

Third-generation laminates

Chapter 4: **Standard Laminate Designs** | 51

Figure 42

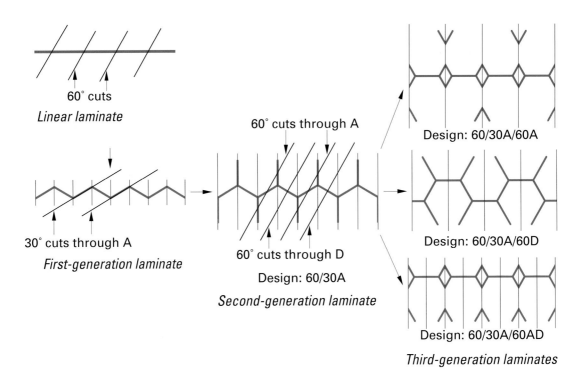

Figure 43

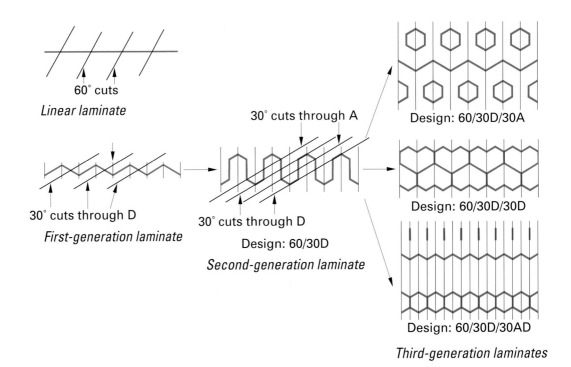

Figure 44

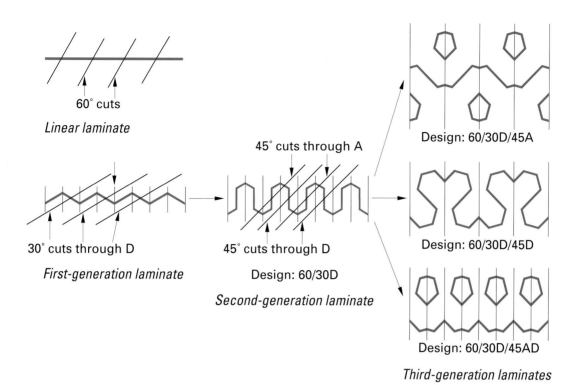

60° cuts

Linear laminate

30° cuts through D

First-generation laminate

45° cuts through A

45° cuts through D

Design: 60/30D

Second-generation laminate

Design: 60/30D/45A

Design: 60/30D/45D

Design: 60/30D/45AD

Third-generation laminates

Figure 45

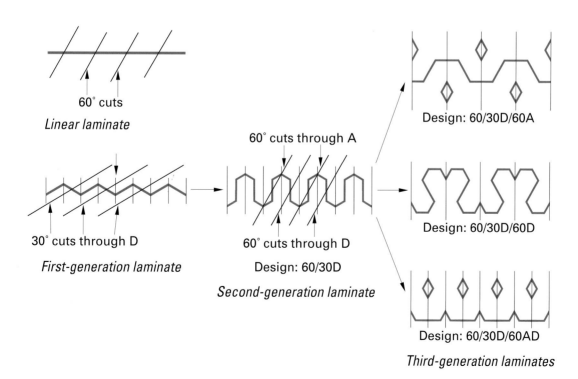

60° cuts

Linear laminate

30° cuts through D

First-generation laminate

60° cuts through A

60° cuts through D

Design: 60/30D

Second-generation laminate

Design: 60/30D/60A

Design: 60/30D/60D

Design: 60/30D/60AD

Third-generation laminates

Figure 46

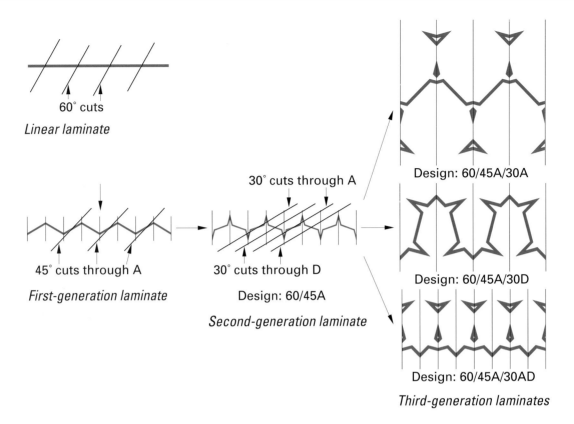

60° cuts

Linear laminate

30° cuts through A

45° cuts through A

First-generation laminate

30° cuts through D

Design: 60/45A

Second-generation laminate

Design: 60/45A/30A

Design: 60/45A/30D

Design: 60/45A/30AD

Third-generation laminates

Figure 47

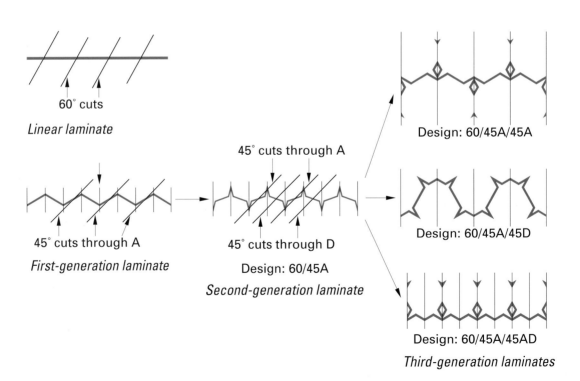

60° cuts

Linear laminate

45° cuts through A

45° cuts through A

First-generation laminate

45° cuts through D

Design: 60/45A

Second-generation laminate

Design: 60/45A/45A

Design: 60/45A/45D

Design: 60/45A/45AD

Third-generation laminates

Figure 48

60° cuts

Linear laminate

60° cuts through A

Design: 60/45A/60A

45° cuts through A

First-generation laminate

60° cuts through D

Design: 60/45A

Second-generation laminate

Design: 60/45A/60D

Design: 60/45A/60AD

Third-generation laminates

Figure 49

60° cuts

Linear laminate

30° cuts through A

Design: 60/45D/30A

45° cuts through D

First-generation laminate

30° cuts through D

Design: 60/45D

Second-generation laminate

Design: 60/45D/30D

Design: 60/45D/30AD

Third-generation laminates

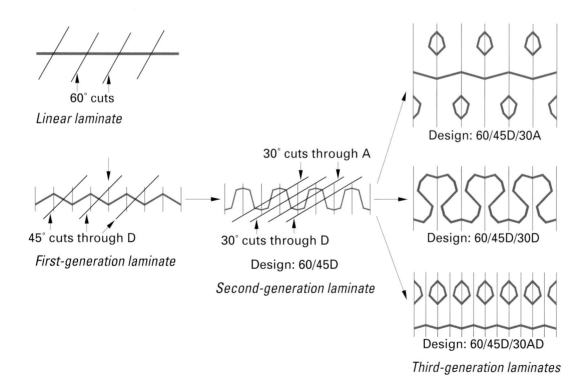

Figure 50

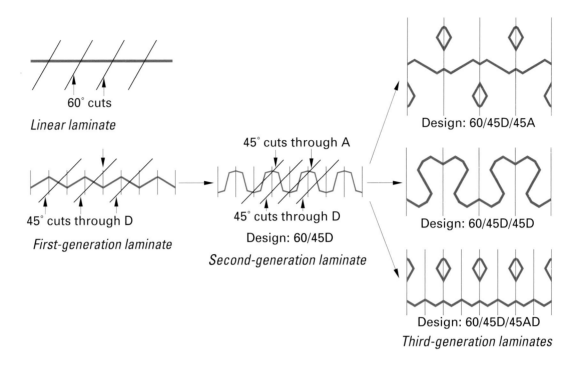

Figure 51

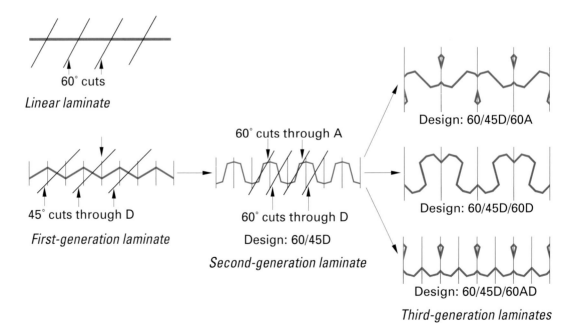

Figure 52

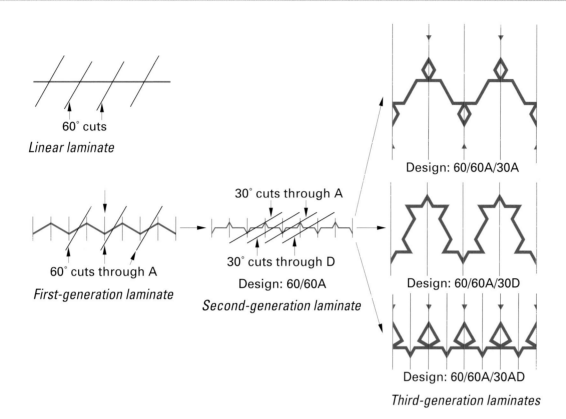

60° cuts
Linear laminate

60° cuts through A
First-generation laminate

30° cuts through A
30° cuts through D
Design: 60/60A
Second-generation laminate

Design: 60/60A/30A

Design: 60/60A/30D

Design: 60/60A/30AD
Third-generation laminates

Figure 53

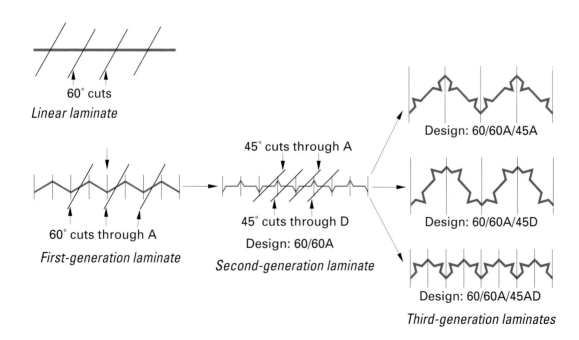

60° cuts
Linear laminate

60° cuts through A
First-generation laminate

45° cuts through A
45° cuts through D
Design: 60/60A
Second-generation laminate

Design: 60/60A/45A

Design: 60/60A/45D

Design: 60/60A/45AD
Third-generation laminates

Chapter 4: **Standard Laminate Designs**

Figure 54

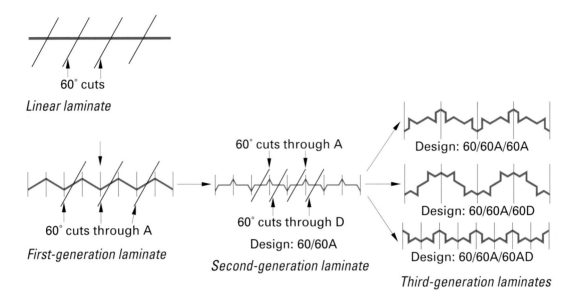

60° cuts

Linear laminate

60° cuts through A

First-generation laminate

60° cuts through A

60° cuts through D

Design: 60/60A

Second-generation laminate

Design: 60/60A/60A

Design: 60/60A/60D

Design: 60/60A/60AD

Third-generation laminates

Figure 55

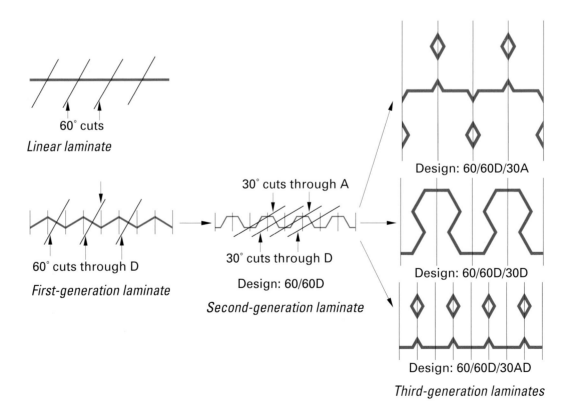

60° cuts

Linear laminate

60° cuts through D

First-generation laminate

30° cuts through A

30° cuts through D

Design: 60/60D

Second-generation laminate

Design: 60/60D/30A

Design: 60/60D/30D

Design: 60/60D/30AD

Third-generation laminates

Figure 56

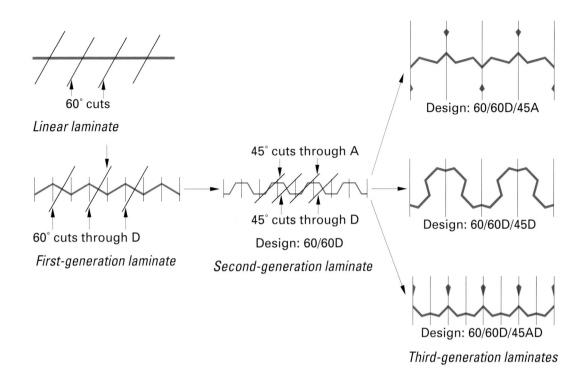

60° cuts

Linear laminate

60° cuts through D

First-generation laminate

45° cuts through A

45° cuts through D

Design: 60/60D

Second-generation laminate

Design: 60/60D/45A

Design: 60/60D/45D

Design: 60/60D/45AD

Third-generation laminates

Figure 57

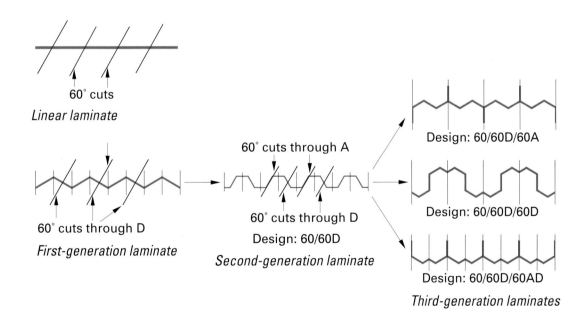

60° cuts

Linear laminate

60° cuts through D

First-generation laminate

60° cuts through A

60° cuts through D

Design: 60/60D

Second-generation laminate

Design: 60/60D/60A

Design: 60/60D/60D

Design: 60/60D/60AD

Third-generation laminates

Figure 58

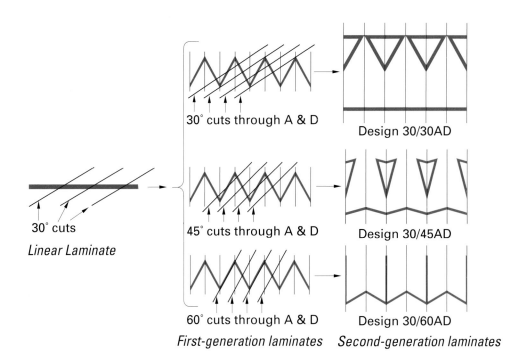

30° cuts

Linear Laminate

30° cuts through A & D

Design 30/30AD

45° cuts through A & D

Design 30/45AD

60° cuts through A & D

Design 30/60AD

First-generation laminates   *Second-generation laminates*

Figure 59

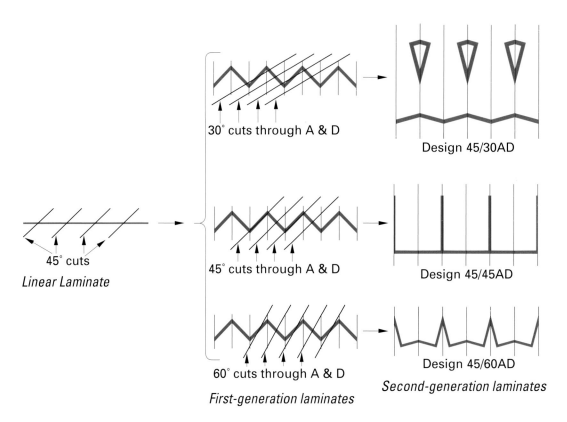

45° cuts

Linear Laminate

30° cuts through A & D

Design 45/30AD

45° cuts through A & D

Design 45/45AD

60° cuts through A & D

Design 45/60AD

First-generation laminates   *Second-generation laminates*

Figure 60

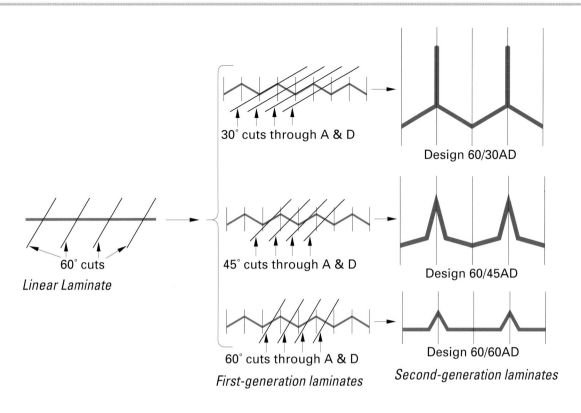

30° cuts through A & D

Design 60/30AD

45° cuts through A & D

Design 60/45AD

60° cuts

Linear Laminate

60° cuts through A & D

First-generation laminates

Design 60/60AD

Second-generation laminates

Figure 61. LINEAR LAMINATE WITH SIMULATED WOOD GRAIN

Figure 62. FIRST-GENERATION LAMINATE WITH ZIGZAG WOOD GRAIN PATTERN AND STRIPE DESIGN

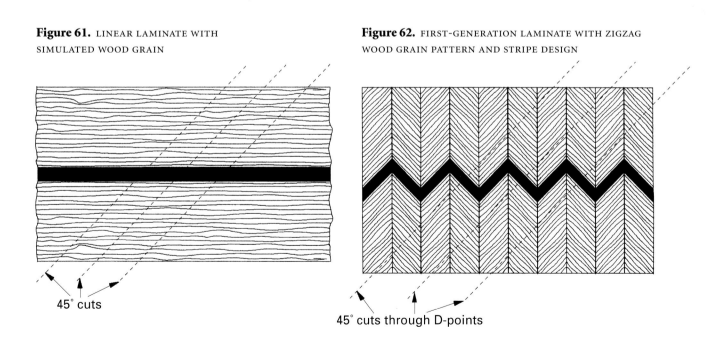

45° cuts

45° cuts through D-points

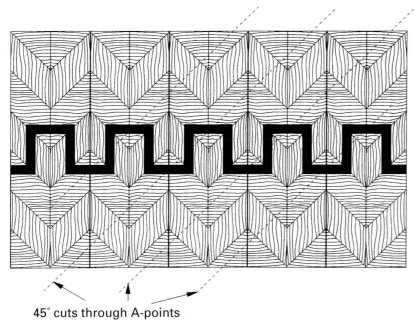

45° cuts through A-points

Figure 63. A SECOND-GENERATION LAMINATE WITH SEVERAL SUBTLE ZIGZAG PATTERNS RESULTING FROM THE WOOD GRAIN

Figure 64. A THIRD-GENERATION LAMINATE WITH SUBTLE DESIGNS RESULTING FROM THE WOOD GRAIN

Chapter 5
Variables in Standard Laminate Design

There are several variables that affect the design or pattern of standard laminates, and each variable can be changed independently to alter the character of the design. Many combinations are possible, because the process can be carried through several stages or generations of laminates.

The variables in the process affect the laminate design in several ways. The size of the pattern—its overall width and height—is largely determined by the width of the cross sections cut from the linear laminate. The height of the design is somewhat dependent on the complexity and width of the stripe. The design configuration results from two independent process variables: cutting angle and cutting location. This chapter contains illustrations that show how the design changes as each variable is changed independently. Note that the thick diagonal black lines represent the cutting

angle and location and the vertical black lines represent glue joints.

A stripe can have many designs, depending on the number and variety of wood strips used in the process. Increasing the number of wood strips increases the complexity and, usually, the height of the design. Figure 1 demonstrates the difference in a mitered laminate design when a narrow, a medium, or a wide stripe is used. In these examples, all of the other variables stay the same, but the character of the final design is quite different. With some patterns, a wider stripe causes the design to separate into elements that are no longer connected to the continuous part of the pattern. In this example, small triangles have separated from the continuous pattern in the laminates that use the medium and wide stripes. The triangles increase in size as the width of the stripe increases.

Figure 1. THE EFFECT OF STRIPE COMPLEXITY ON MITERED LAMINATE DESIGNS

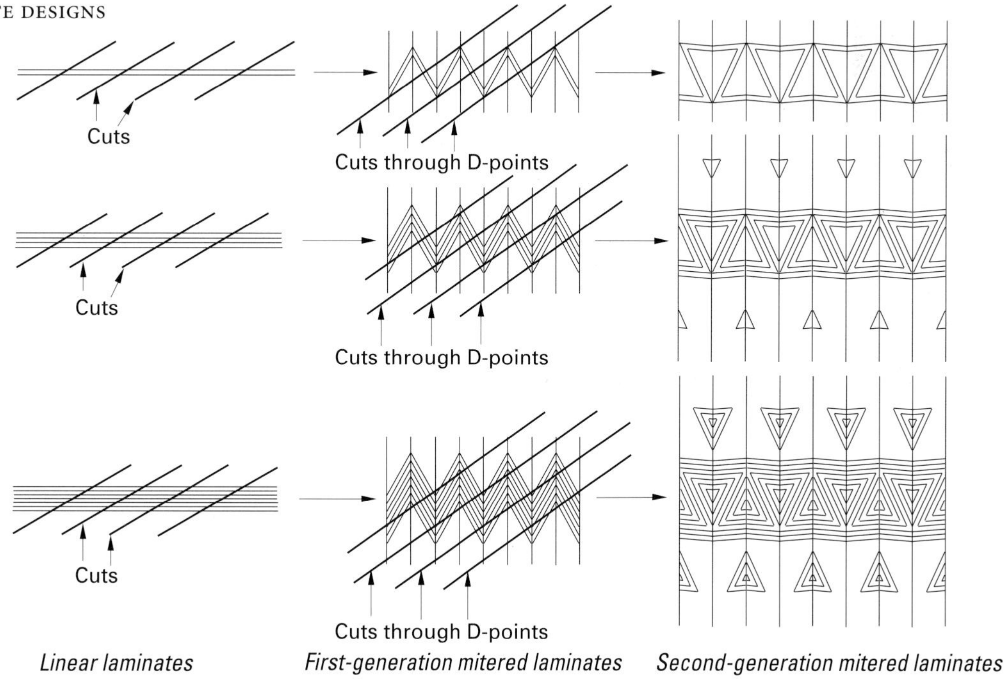

Linear laminates — First-generation mitered laminates — Second-generation mitered laminates

The length and width of each repeating unit depend on the width of the initial cross sections cut from the linear laminate. This also governs the width of every cross section that is cut from any succeeding generation of mitered laminate, because the width of these cross sections is not optional. All standard mitered laminates (not including the linear laminate) are cut through the midpoint of either the ascending legs, descending legs, or both legs of the pattern. Doubling the width of the sections doubles the size of the design.

Figure 2 shows the stripe in magenta. Doubling the size of the cross sections carries through to all the succeeding generations of laminates. For example, the width of the initial cross sections cut from the linear laminate determines the size of the next-generation laminates; it affects the overall size of the design, but not the general course or direction. How to calculate the size of any design based on the width of the initial cross sections is detailed in chapter 9.

The course or direction of the design is changed significantly, however, by two other variables—the angle and the specific midpoint at which a mitered laminate is cut. The cutting angle is a continuous variable. Theoretically, it can be any angle between 0° and 90°. Changing the cutting angle at any stage in the process will alter the design. Figure 3 illustrates the changes in design that occur when a first-generation pattern is cut into sections at seven different angles. These are then glued together into second-generation laminates. Going from 22½° to 67½° makes a dramatic difference by changing only one variable. Small changes in angle cause only minor variations in the design, though larger changes can alter the overall characteristics of the pattern.

Several generalizations can be drawn from examining these seven second-generation designs. Three distinct types of patterns are produced. One merges into the other at critical points in the process. The small angle (22½°) results in the narrowest cross sections. The width of the cross sections increases progressively when going from the lower to the higher angle. Also, the height of the overall design decreases, becoming rather flat at the largest angle. The four-sided, disconnected figures are quite wide at the lower angle but get narrower as the angle increases, converging into a line at the 45° cutting angle. The lines become points that get less sharp as the angle increases. These changes are rather typical for mitered laminates. For a demonstration of how the design is affected by varying the cutting angle, see chapter 4 (Figures 4 through 60).

Figure 2. THE EFFECT THE THICKNESS OF CROSS SECTIONS HAS ON THE SIZE OF MITERED LAMINATE DESIGNS

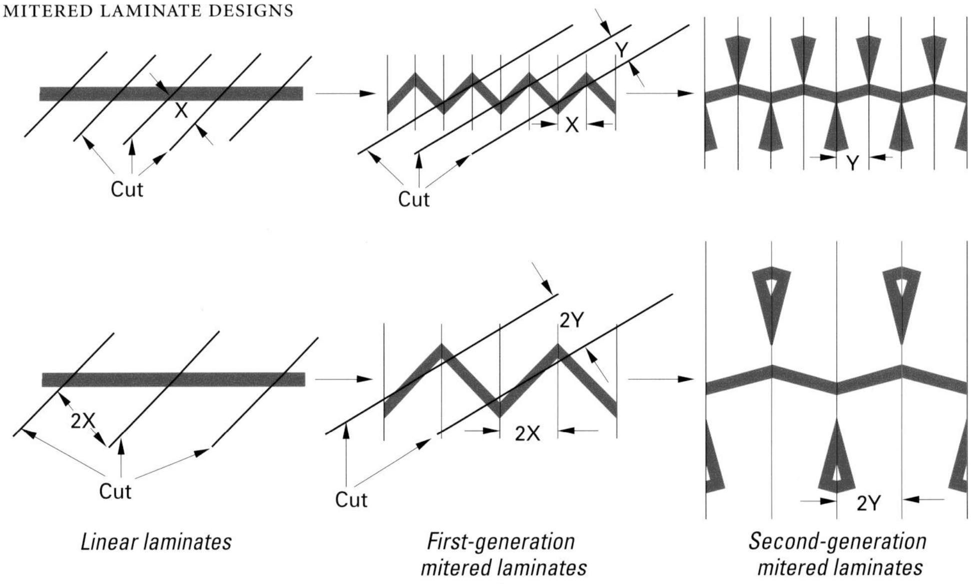

Linear laminates   *First-generation mitered laminates*   *Second-generation mitered laminates*

Figure 3. THE EFFECT OF THE CUTTING ANGLE ON MITERED LAMINATE DESIGNS

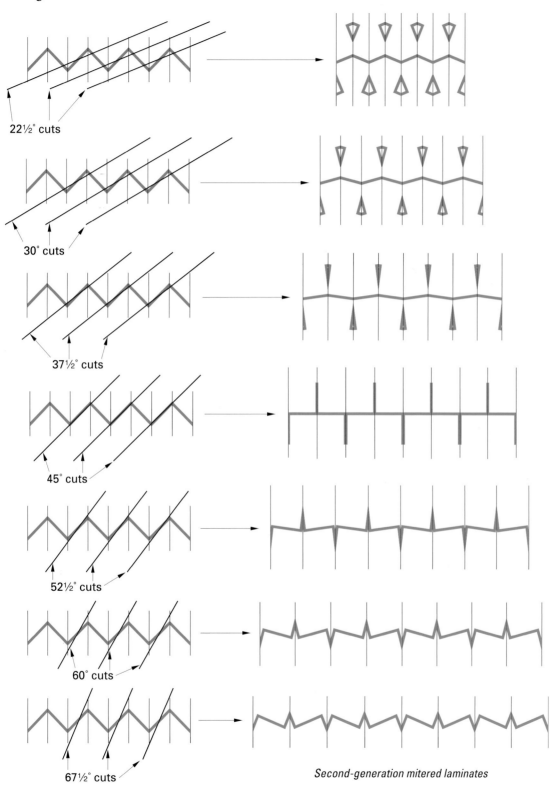

22½° cuts

30° cuts

37½° cuts

45° cuts

52½° cuts

60° cuts

67½° cuts

First-generation mitered laminates

Second-generation mitered laminates

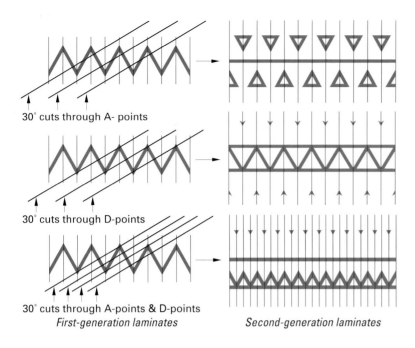

30° cuts through A-points

30° cuts through D-points

30° cuts through A-points & D-points

First-generation laminates   *Second-generation laminates*

Figure 4. THE EFFECT OF THE CUTTING POINT ON MITERED LAMINATE DESIGNS

The other variable that dramatically affects the design is the point at which the laminate is cut. There are only two such points (A-points and D-points) when making standard patterns. Two distinct designs are created when one or the other of these points is cut, and a third design is created when both points are cut. Figure 4 depicts the three distinct patterns that are made from a single laminate at one cutting angle. (This was also illustrated in Figures 4 through 60 in chapter 4.) At any angle, three different patterns can be achieved. As a result, many patterns can be made from any one mitered laminate.

Though this chapter has discussed how changing one variable at a time can affect a pattern, all of these variables can be applied simultaneously. With this in mind, it is not difficult to imagine the large number of designs that can be created. Some of the designs will be similar, but there also will be dramatic differences. Only a small number of these, around 200, are illustrated in this book.

Photo 1. BOWL MADE BY THE SEGMENTED RING METHOD; 9¼ X 4 INCHES (23.5 X 10 CM); WALNUT, MAPLE, MAHOGANY, AND TWO UNKNOWN WOOD SPECIES

Photo 2. A SECOND-GENERATION MITERED LAMINATE TRAY MADE USING THE STANDARD METHOD; 18 X 12 X 2½ INCHES (45.5 X 30.5 X 6.5 CM); WALNUT, POPLAR, AND ONE UNKNOWN SPECIES

Chapter 6
Nonlinear Designs

Up to this point, I have discussed only linear laminates and linear mitered laminates. The standard process starts with a linear laminate and produces a linear mitered laminate. The term *linear* refers to the stripe in the initial laminate and to the design in all other laminates. It means that the design goes from one point to another point in a straight line and in a single plane. When either is not true, it is *nonlinear*. In other words, in a linear laminate, the stripe and design are both linear, but in a linear mitered laminate, only the design is linear. In this chapter, various types of nonlinear designs and how they are made from linear ones are discussed.

Planar Mitered Laminate Design

There are two general types of structural shapes that can be enhanced with mitered laminates. The first type is *planar mitered laminate designs*, in which the mitered laminate design is all in one plane. The other type is *peripheral laminate designs*, in which the laminate design is curved to fit the periphery of a cylinder. Planar mitered laminate designs can be further divided into three categories: *linear*, *angular*, and *curved*. Planar linear designs have been thoroughly discussed in the prior chapters. Thus, only the last two are covered below.

ANGULAR LAMINATES

If a linear mitered laminate design is altered so that the design changes direction, it becomes an angular design. In angular designs, a linear laminate design is joined to another design that runs in a different direction. Angular design can be made by four procedures, each producing a design that is different at the junction where the two linear mitered laminate sections are joined. Three of these methods are accomplished by cutting a planar laminate at an angle. The fourth method, called the *conversion pieces method*, does not involve cutting. It is made by using a mixture of cross sections from two generations of mitered laminates.

There are three ways to cut a laminate to form an angular design, each producing a different design at the mitered joint: two variations of the *single-cut method* and the *double-cut method*. In making an angled laminate by a cutting method, the mitered ends of two mitered laminates are glued together. When joined, the design must match or line up on either side of the glued joint and must change direction at this joint; but the cuts can be made at any angle.

In the first variation of the single-cut method, a cut is made through the A-point of a mitered laminate. Use the same procedure as was detailed for cutting a cross section from a linear mitered laminate (see chapter 3). The angled laminate is made by turning one end of this cut laminate over, placing its cut edge against the cut edge of the other piece, and gluing the two pieces together. The design must match at the joint. Figure 1 shows the cut going through the A-point (upper left corner) and (below and to the right) the design that is produced by this procedure.

In the other variation of the single-cut method, the cut is made through the D-point in the same manner. Figure 2 shows the results obtained by using this method. Note that the designs at the junction of the two sections of laminate are not the same. The mitered joint shown in Photo 1 was cut at 45° through the D-point.

In the double-cut method, two cuts are made through the mitered laminate. The cuts must go through corresponding points. There are many such points in a mitered laminate. Corresponding points are the only combination of two points where the resulting design will match or line up on both sides of the mitered joint. The cuts are made in the same way as described earlier in this book (see page 26). An example of making cuts through two corresponding points in a laminate and the resulting angular laminate design are shown in Figure 3. Note that the design at the joint is different from the designs in either Figure 1 or Figure 2.

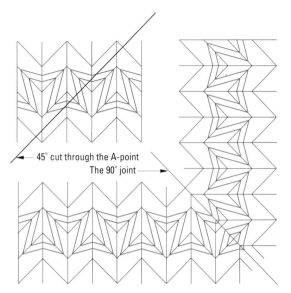

Figure 1. CUTTING A SECOND-GENERATION MITERED LAMINATE THROUGH THE A-POINTS FOR A 90° CORNER

Figure 2. CUTTING A SECOND-GENERATION MITERED LAMINATE THROUGH THE D-POINTS FOR A 90° CORNER

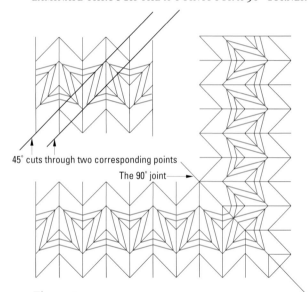

Figure 3. CUTTING A SECOND-GENERATION MITERED LAMINATE THROUGH TWO CORRESPONDING POINTS FOR A 90° CORNER

Photo 1. THIS CORNER OF A SECOND-GENERATION DESIGN, WHICH WAS INCORPORATED AS A BORDER INTO A GAME TABLE, IS ONE RESULT OF MAKING A CORNER USING THE SINGLE-CUT METHOD. THE CUT WAS MADE THROUGH THE D-POINT AT A 45° ANGLE.

In comparing the single-cut and double-cut methods, each one has advantages over the other. The single-cut method requires only one cut so there is no loss of laminate. So why choose the double-cut method? In the double-cut method, there are no restrictions on the distance between two angles in a mitered laminate design (or the length of straight side in a figure), since you have the option of choosing any location to make the two corresponding cuts. For example, the sides of a rectangle made with a mitered laminate can be any length. With the single-cut method, cuts can be made only at incremental points (either A-points or D-points) along the design.

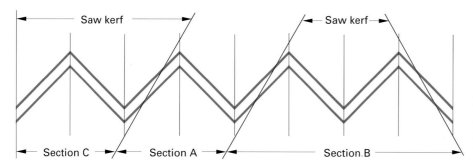

Figure 4. HOW TO CUT A FIRST-GENERATION LAMINATE INTO SECTIONS FOR A RIGHT-ANGLE CORNER

The conversion pieces method of making an angled mitered laminate does not require a special cut through a mitered laminate. The change in direction is brought about by gluing together a combination of cross sections cut from two different generations of laminates. It is easier to illustrate the process than to describe it. Figure 4 illustrates how sections are cut from a first-generation laminate into three different configurations. Section A is the same as a cross section cut for a second-generation laminate. Sections B and C are two different first-generation laminate sections. These sections have been combined in Figure 5 (note that two A-sections were used) so that the design changes from a horizontal to a vertical direction. The design is actually one-quarter of the whole design used in making the tray in chapter 12 (see page 125).

Angled mitered laminates can be made in a variety of configurations. The size of the angle, the length of section between joints, and the relative orientation of each section can be varied. The angle of a joint or corner is twice that of the cutting angle. A small-angle cut produces a very sharp or small-joint angle. For example, to make 90° corners, cut the mitered laminate ends at 45°. For 60° corners, make 30° cuts across the laminate.

Angled joints can be made at both ends of a section of mitered laminate. Two or more of these can be glued together, thus producing a design with several angled turns. These can be open-ended, or the two ends can be joined to form a closed figure. Examples of closed figures are any figure with straight sides—triangles, squares, rectangles, parallelograms, rhomboids, and so forth.

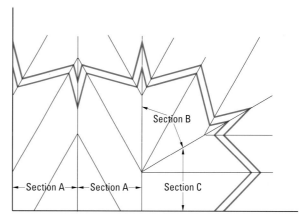

Figure 5. HOW FOUR TRANSITIONAL PIECES CUT FROM A FIRST-GENERATION LAMINATE ARE COMBINED INTO ONE QUADRANT OF THE TRAY DESIGN. NOTE THAT THE CORNERS ARE NOT SYMMETRICAL.

A surface can be enhanced with a combination of different designs, linear variations, and configurations. Two or more planar linear mitered laminates can be glued together side by side and used in a project. An example is the cutting board in chapter 2 (page 17, Photo 2, left), which shows three designs (two of which are the same) that go from one end of the board to the other. A more complex design, which is planar but nonlinear, is the game-table top shown in chapter 12 (page 132). It has a square (angular) design as a border, a circular (curved) design in the center, and, in between, an octagonal (angular) design. Many other combinations are possible.

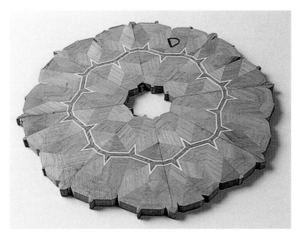

Photo 2. THIS CIRCULAR DESIGN MADE FROM WEDGES CUT FROM A FIRST-GENERATION MITERED LAMINATE WAS USED AS THE CENTRAL DESIGN FOR A GAME TABLE.

Photo 3. BOWL MADE BY USING THE MITERED LAMINATE PROCESS WITH A NONSTANDARD DESIGN ON THE SIDES AND SECOND-GENERATION DESIGN IN THE BOTTOM, 9½ X 3⅛ INCHES (23.5 X 7.8 CM); SEVEN UNKNOWN WOOD SPECIES

CURVED LAMINATES

If the sections of linear mitered laminates are short and joined so that the changes in direction are small, the resulting design simulates a curve. This is called a *curved planar mitered laminate*. Any type of curve or combination of curves can be made by varying the cutting angles and the length of mitered laminate sections. Circular, oval, and other closed designs can be made by joining the ends of the curved sections. Sections of curved designs can be combined with linear or angular mitered laminate designs in many combinations. For example, a rectangle with rounded corners could be made.

The central design in the top of the game table (see Photo 2, opposite, and chapter 12, page 132) and in the bottom of the bowl (Photo 3) are two examples of circular designs. The circular design in the drawing in Figure 7 is very similar and illustrates the process of making curved designs. This circular laminate is made from a second-generation linear mitered laminate, though any type of laminate can be used.

The laminate is cut into sectors, wedges, or pie-shaped pieces on the sliding table cutoff jig with a centering attachment (described in chapter 3). To cut sectors so that 12 (any number could have been chosen) will fit together into a circular disk, set and adjust the angle fence at 15° [½ (360°/12) = 15°]. Cut off the end of the laminate, making the cut through either an A-point or a D-point. Figure 6 illustrates the location of successive cuts when made through the D-points. All subsequent cuts are made through the same point. Turn the laminate upside down and make a cut through the next (but the same) center point in the design. This produces the first sector in which the angle between its cut edges is 30°.

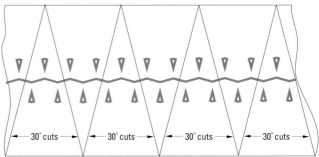

Figure 6. CUTTING A SECOND-GENERATION MITERED LAMINATE INTO 30° WEDGES USED FOR MAKING A CIRCULAR DESIGN

Photo 4. BOWLS: LEFT, FIRST-GENERATION DESIGN, 8¼ X 1 INCHES (21 X 2.5 CM), MAPLE, CHERRY, AND WALNUT; TOP, SECOND-GENERATION DESIGN, 11½ X 1¼ INCHES (29 X 3 CM), REDWOOD AND RED OAK; BOTTOM, NOT A MITERED LAMINATE DESIGN, 10½ X 1 INCHES (26.5 X 2.5 CM), HARD MAPLE AND WALNUT

For the second sector, again turn the laminate up-side down and cut through the next center point. Make additional sectors in the same way, turning the laminate over between every cut. Glue 12 of these sectors together into a circular design, using a circular clamp to hold them in place while the glue dries. How these 12 sectors fit together into a circular design is shown in Figure 7.

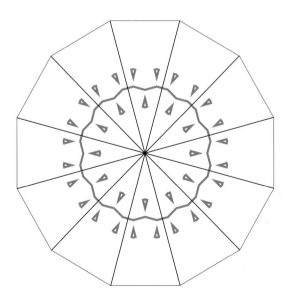

Figure 7. HOW 12 OF THE 30° WEDGES MAKE A CIRCULAR DESIGN

Converting a linear mitered laminate into a circular laminate by the above procedure does not change the design—the circular design is the same as the linear one. When a laminate is repeatedly cut through successive center points, every cut produces a sector. In other words, each cut makes a matching edge on each of two sectors. Sectors can also be made in which the cuts do not go through one of the center points. The design can be cut at any location, but the next cut must be made through a corresponding point. However, this requires two cuts for every sector, since each cut produces only one edge that can be matched up with another sector. This method results in some loss of laminate, and there is a change in the resulting design at the joint.

Any of the planar laminates discussed above can be converted into structural forms with contoured surfaces. The most common method is to shape the laminates with a lathe. Any planar laminate can be turned on the lathe into a circular shape such as a plate, a platter, a round plaque, a shallow bowl, or a round trivet, and so forth. Photos 4 , 5, and 6 show several designs that have been turned on a lathe. (The plate in the bottom center of Photo 4 was made from a laminate made by using the band saw method.) The only requirement is that the linear mitered laminate must be at least as thick as the depth or height of the item that is made from it. For example, if the laminate is 2 inches (5 cm) thick, it can be turned into a bowl that is just under 2 inches (5 cm) deep.

Photo 5. BOWL MADE BY USING THE MITERED
LAMINATE PROCESS WITH A SECOND-GENERATION
DESIGN; 7⅜ X 2¼ INCHES (19 X 5.5 CM); HARD MAPLE,
RED MAPLE, AND WALNUT

Photo 6. PLATE MADE BY USING THE MITERED
LAMINATE PROCESS WITH A FIRST-GENERATION
DESIGN; 16½ X 1⅛ INCHES (42 X 2.8 CM); MAPLE,
WALNUT, AND CHERRY

Peripheral Mitered Laminate Designs

If the design is not in the same plane, but goes around the periphery of a cylinder or sphere, it becomes a *peripheral mitered laminate design*. A linear mitered laminate can be converted into a tall circular structure in which the laminate design goes around the periphery. This is a peripheral mitered laminate. Unlike the limitations on the height or depth of a turned linear mitered laminate, these structures can be made to any reasonable height or depth. They are made from cross sections cut from a linear laminate in which both edges of each cross section are made with a compound miter rather than a simple miter cut. These are then fitted and glued together into a hollow cylinder in which the laminate design encircles the periphery of the cylinder.

A disk can be glued to this hollow cylinder to serve as the bottom of the piece. Then, the structure is turned on a lathe into a bowl with a continuous design going around the sides of the bowl. If two of these cylinders are glued together (into a longer hollow cylinder) with a round disk for a bottom, the structure can be turned into a vase with two peripheral laminated designs. By gluing a round disk to one end of such a cylinder and a cylindrical-shaped block of wood to the other, the combined shapes can be converted into a bottle with a neck (chapter 1, Photo 13). Many other types of vessels can be made using this method.

These peripheral mitered laminates can be made by two methods. One is the *peripheral generation-conversion method* and the other is simply the *peripheral conversion method*. In these processes, the cross sections, when fitted and glued together, become the walls of a hollow cylinder. In the generation-conversion process, the cross sections must be cut so that, when fitted together and glued, the linear mitered laminate is converted into the next-generation laminate (with a change in design) and, at the same time, into a round shell structure with straight sides.

Figure 8. HOW A LINEAR FIRST-GENERATION MITERED LAMINATE IS CUT INTO CROSS SECTIONS WITH COMPOUND MITERS

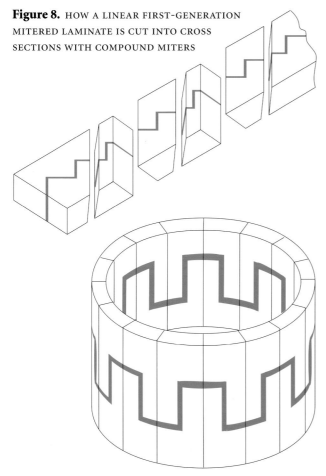

Figure 9. A HOLLOW CYLINDER FORMED FROM 16 COMPOUND-MITERED CROSS SECTIONS

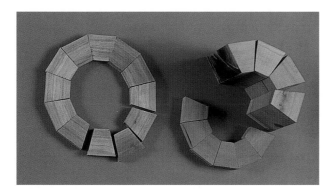

Photo 7. THE TWO TYPES OF COMPOUND-MITER-CUT CROSS SECTIONS FOR THE SIDES OF THE VASE IN PHOTO 18 (PAGE 78) ARE STACKED INTO A CIRCLE PRIOR TO BEING GLUED INTO TWO CIRCULAR CONFIGURATIONS.

This means that the cross sections must be cut with compound miters. The drawing in Figure 8 illustrates how the cross sections are mitered. Figure 9 shows these cross sections glued into a hollow cylinder. In this drawing, the sharp ends of the cross sections have been cut off. As in converting any laminate to the next generation, all cuts must be made through either an A-point or a D-point, or both. See also Photo 7.

These compound miter cuts are made with the sliding table cutoff jig with the centering attachment (see pages 27 and 28). To make these cuts, though, some changes have to be made. The angle fence must be extended into the upper right corner of the sliding table jig. Every other cut through the laminate must be made with the laminate positioned against the fence in the upper right section of the table jig. The extended fence is set and adjusted for the angle required for the particular design to be made.

The other angle is made by tilting the saw blade. The amount of tilt is based on the number of cross sections needed for making the hollow cylinder. If 16 sectors are needed for making the cylinder, for example, set the tilt at ½ (360°/16) or 11¼° from up and down. This angle must be accurately set so the joints between the sections fit perfectly. Perform practice cuts, using scrap wood, until the exact angle is achieved.

Positioning the laminate to make these mitered cuts requires more skill than cutting cross sections from mitered laminates. In making standard mitered laminates, cuts must go through the exact center of a leg of the design. The exact center point is actually in the middle of the laminate, halfway between the top and bottom surfaces. When making planar laminates, cuts are made at right angles to the upper face or surface of the laminate design. The same cut goes through the exact center of the pattern on the bottom face of the design as well as the middle part.

When the cut is made at an angle other then 90°, the cut goes through the design at different points along its length. If the saw blade is tilted to the left, a cut through the exact central point of the design will cut the design to the left of center on the top surface of the laminate and to the right of center on the bottom. The reverse is true if the saw blade is tilted to the right. However, corresponding points on the design on the upper faces must still be used as guides in centering the laminate when cutting the sections. The saw cut through the top face of the laminate must be offset slightly from its center point so that the saw will go through the exact center of the pattern. To use the corresponding points as a guide, the pair of wires or scribed lines, depending on which attachment jig is used, must also be offset or shifted slightly. This offset can be calculated. However, practice cuts are usually still required. It is more prudent to do the positioning by trial and error from the beginning. The aim is to make the cut so that when the cutoff cross section is turned over and its cut edge is held against the cut edge of the laminate, the design on one side of the joint is a mirror image of the design on the other side. The design must match on both faces of the joined laminate. If the two designs do not match perfectly, the centering attachment must be adjusted accordingly.

Having extended and set the angle fence, set the saw blade tilt, properly adjust the centering attachment, and place the laminate against the angle fence in the lower left quadrant of the table. Position the corresponding points on the laminate design underneath the wires or the lines on the plastic triangles. Clamp and cut off the end of the laminate. As described above, check the cut for accuracy, adjusting the positioning jig if necessary. Unclamp and position the laminate against the angle fence in the upper right part of the sliding jig. After positioning the corresponding points underneath the guide wires or lines, clamp, and cut off the first cross section.

Reposition the laminate against the fence in the lower left quadrant of the sliding jig. Repeat the positioning, clamping, and cutting to produce the second section. Repeat the above steps, alternating the position of the laminate from the lower left part of the sliding jig to the upper right area. Cut the number of sections required for a complete hollow cylinder. Glue these together, using circular clamps, matching the design at every glued joint. The hollow cylinder can be glued to a block of wood and turned into a bowl. It can also be glued to other solid or hollow cylinders and turned into a vase, urn, or bottle. The design in the turned item runs all the way around the periphery of the turned object, as well as through the thickness of its wall (Photo 9).

In the simple conversion method, the cross sections are made with simple miter cuts. The cross sections are cut at right angles to the longitudinal axis of a linear mitered laminate, but the saw blade must be tilted so that the cross sections are made with mitered cut edges, similar to the edges on a barrel stave. The resulting mitered laminate design varies, depending on where these cuts are made. If these cuts are made through either the A-points or the D-points, the laminate design in the converted structure closely resembles the one in the original planar laminate. If, however, the cuts are made through both of these points, the resulting laminate has an AD-design. This procedure converts either an A-laminate or a D-laminate into a laminate with the same AD-design. For example, either a 30/45A or a 30/45D linear mitered laminate produces a 30/45AD peripheral mitered laminate. See chapter 7 for details on coding laminates.

In the simple peripheral conversion method, the procedure for making the cuts through the linear mitered laminate is the same for both variations except, in this case, all the cuts are made in the lower left quadrant of the sliding table cutoff jig. The angle fence is set at 90° to the saw blade. The saw blade is tilted at an angle corresponding to the number of cross sections required for the peripheral design. (The angle is calculated in the same manner as described above, and the centering attachment is adjusted as described above for cutting compound mitered cross sections for a peripheral design.) It must be adjusted so that when the cutoff section is turned over and placed against the cut end, the two designs match. If they do not match, the attachment must be adjusted until they do.

The first cut is made with the linear mitered laminate facing up. The second cut is made with the laminate turned upside down. For the third cut, the laminate is again turned face up. The laminate is thus turned over between every cut. The cut sections are assembled, matched up, and glued together into a hollow cylinder. Thus, the design encircles the cylinder.

PICTURING THE PROCESS

The complete process of making a peripheral laminate is shown in Photos 8 through 18. Photo 8 shows a linear laminate being cut into sections for a first-generation laminate. If the cuts had been made with compound miters, the sections could have been converted to a first-generation peripheral design, such as the large one on the vase in Photo 9.

Photo 10 shows the conversion of a first-generation laminate into a second-generation design on a cutoff jig.

Photo 8. CUTTING THE LINEAR LAMINATE INTO CROSS SECTIONS TO BE USED IN MAKING A FIRST-GENERATION LAMINATE DESIGN

Photo 9. A VASE MADE FROM COMPOUND-MITER-CUT CROSS SECTIONS MADE FROM TWO DIFFERENT LINEAR LAMINATES, WHICH WERE LAYERED TO FORM TWO FIRST-GENERATION PERIPHERAL DESIGNS; 6¾ X 12½ INCHES (17 X 31.5 CM); WALNUT AND MAPLE. ANY NUMBER OF LAMINATES CAN BE GLUED TOGETHER IN ONE VESSEL IN THIS MANNER.

Part of this second-generation laminate was used to make a cutting board with a linear mitered laminate design. A border is being glued to the laminate in Photo 11. The completed board is shown in Photo 12, left.

Photo 10. CUTTING THE FIRST-GENERATION LAMINATE INTO CROSS SECTIONS, WHICH WILL BE GLUED TOGETHER INTO A SECOND-GENERATION LAMINATE (SEE LOWER RIGHT OF PHOTO)

Photo 11. GLUING A MITERED WALNUT BORDER TO A PIECE OF SECOND-GENERATION LAMINATE TO MAKE A CUTTING BOARD

Photo 12. CUTTING BOARDS: LEFT, A SECOND-GENERATION DESIGN, 15¼ X 10¼ X ⅞ INCH (38.5 X 26 X 2.2 CM) IN WALNUT, CHERRY, AND POPLAR; RIGHT, MADE WITH THREE NONSTANDARD MITERED LAMINATE DESIGNS (ACROSS CENTER AND ENDS) AND TWO IDENTICAL DESIGNS MADE BY THE BLOCKING, LAYERING, OR TIERING METHOD, 15¾ X 10½ X ⅞ INCH (40 X 27 X 2.2 CM) IN MAPLE, POPLAR, CHERRY, AND FOUR UNKNOWN WOOD SPECIES

The remainder of the laminate is converted to third-generation cross sections with mitered edges (Photo 13). These are then arranged and glued into a cylindrical configuration with the design encircling the periphery of the structure as depicted in Photo 14. This cylindrical shape will be made into the top half of a vase and a similar one cut from a piece of solid wood will be used for the bottom half of the vase.

After cutting off and leveling the ends of the cylindrical shapes, two sectored rings are glued to one end of the upper cylinder and will become its top opening (Photo 15)

Photo 13. CUTTING THE SECOND-GENERATION LAMINATE INTO COMPOUND-MITERED, THIRD-GENERATION CROSS SECTIONS, WHICH FORM A HOLLOW CYLINDRICAL SHELL WHEN FITTED TOGETHER

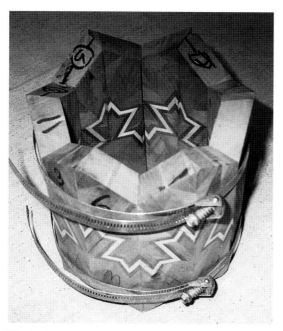

Photo 14. CLAMPING THE GLUED AND MITERED THIRD-GENERATION CROSS SECTIONS INTO A HOLLOW CYLINDER

Photo 15. GLUING THE THIRD-GENERATION HOLLOW CYLINDER (IN A BOWL CLAMP) TO A WALNUT AND A CHERRY WOODEN RING

Photo 16 shows a bottom being glued to one end of the lower cylinder.

The two halves of the vase are turned on the lathe to the desired shape then glued together (Photo 17). Photo 18 shows the finished vase.

Photo 16. GLUING A HOLLOW CHERRY CYLINDER TO A RING OF GLUED-TOGETHER CIRCULAR WALNUT SEGMENTS AND A WALNUT DISK

Photo 17. AFTER SHAPING THE OUTSIDE AND INSIDE SURFACES OF THE UPPER AND LOWER HALVES OF THE VASE ON THE LATHE, THE TWO HALVES ARE GLUED TOGETHER.

Photo 18. VASE MADE WITH A THIRD-GENERATION DESIGN; $13\frac{1}{2}$ X 5 INCHES (34 X 12.5 CM); WALNUT, CHERRY, AND MAPLE

Chapter 7
Identifying Standard Designs

Nearly 200 standard mitered laminate designs are presented in this book. This number includes all the designs made with all combinations of three cutting angles, two cutting locations, three generations of mitered laminates, and one stripe design. As explained in chapter 2, either increasing the number of cutting angles or moving to higher generations increases the number of designs dramatically. In addition, with a second stripe design, the number of laminate designs doubles. Simply changing the width of the stripe also produces a new set of designs.

Chapter 5 showed how making a minor change in the mitered laminate process can make an enormous difference in the final design. The number of designs equals the number of designs possible with a particular stripe multiplied by the number of different stripe designs. Because the number of stripe designs can be very large, the resulting number of possible mitered laminate designs becomes almost limitless.

Sketching Designs

With so many designs, you may wonder how it is possible to communicate information about a design or how one design can be differentiated from another. Indeed, describing a design can be very difficult. The information that is normally needed about a design is what the design looks like and how is it made. It is useful to create a visual model of the design—a sketch or drawing of the design. A drawing shows the path or track of the design parts, the strips in the stripe, and even their arrangement and widths. Labeling identifies the wood species used for each strip. This method provides considerable information about the design.

What a drawing or picture does not show is how the design is created. However, this can be readily portrayed with a code, but in previous chapters, the code was given but not explained. Each design requires a paragraph or two to describe. Although this is easy for a few designs, it becomes very tedious and repetitious when many designs (and generations) are involved. I found that a shorthand method for expressing this information was needed, so I devised one that has been useful to me. This, along with a drawing of the design, is all you will need to duplicate any design.

Photo 1. THE SECOND-GENERATION LAMINATE IN THIS TRAY WAS USED TO MAKE THE THIRD-GENERATION CUTTING BOARD IN PHOTO 5 IN CHAPTER 2 (RIGHT); 17½ X 12 X 2½ INCHES (44.5 X 30.5 X 6.5 CM); WALNUT, MAPLE, AND CHERRY

Coding Standard Designs

My shorthand system or code describes both the composition of the linear laminate and how a mitered laminate is made from it. This information is all contained in a single code line. It is only applicable to a standard laminate; it can not be used for nonstandard designs. The first part of the code describes the variables used in making the linear laminate; the rest describes the variables for converting this to a mitered laminate. Below is an example of a complete code for making a mitered laminate:

(3/16C)(1/8M)2 1/2W (23/32)45/30A/75D

The above is the code for the third-generation design in the square cutting board (see Photo 5 [right], chapter 2). This design was converted from the second-generation laminate that was used for the eight-sided laminate in the game table on page 132 and for the tray on page 79.

Although this code looks very complex, each number, letter, and character has a meaning and, once you familiarize yourself with the format, you will find the code very useful. This particular code describes a third-generation laminate made from a linear laminate with a three-strip stripe. The first part of the code specifies the order and the width of each wood species in the linear laminate. Each set of parentheses represents the specific characteristics for each piece of wood in the stripe. The number gives the width of the strip while the letter is a code for the species of wood used for that strip.

See Table 1 for a list of codes for the more common species of wood. Wood species other than the ones in the table can be identified by their abbreviations or full names. Note that the strip widths are given in inches in this example. You can also use metric measurements, depending on your preferred system.

The information about each strip is given in order. The first set of parentheses lists the variables for the center strip. The second set gives the information for each of the two strips next to the center strip. The specifics for the pair of strips next in line to the above would be listed within the third set of parentheses. Additional pairs of strips are defined in the same manner and order. Thus, the information for the pair of strips farthest from the center strip would be given within the last set of parentheses.

WOOD SPECIES	LETTER CODE	WOOD SPECIES	LETTER CODE
ash	A	mesquite	Ms
beech	Be	monkey pod	Mp
birch	B	oak	O
bocote	Bc	paduak	Pd
bubinga	Bb	pecan	Pc
cedar	Cd	pine	P
cherry	C	poplar	Pp
cocobolo	Cb	purple heart	Ph
ebony	Eb	redwood	R
elm	E	rosewood	Rw
hickory	H	sapele	S
holly	Hy	teak	T
koa	K	walnut	W
luan	L	wenge	Wg
mahogany	Mh	zebrawood	Z
maple	M	ziricote	Zc

Table 1. LETTER CODES FOR WOOD SPECIES

Photo 2. BOWL MADE BY THE SEGMENTED RING METHOD; 9 X 4 INCHES (23 X 10 CM); MAPLE, WALNUT, CHERRY, AND THREE UNKNOWN WOOD SPECIES

The width (again, in inches) and wood species (see Table 1) for the two outboard planks are given next. This number and letter(s) are not enclosed in parentheses and are listed in the code following the last set of parentheses. This completes all the variable information required for making a linear laminate.

The remainder of the code lists the variables needed to make a particular mitered laminate. The variables are listed in the same order as the steps in the process of making the laminate. Two variables, where to cut and at what angle, are required to define how each generation of laminate is made. The generations are separated by forward slashes.

To make the first-generation laminate, the first number specifies how thick to cut each cross section from the linear laminate. This value here, given in inches, is enclosed in parentheses. This thickness determines the overall size of the laminate. The next number is the angle for cutting the linear laminate. The slash following these two numbers shows that the variables for the first-generation laminate have been specified.

The next number and letter(s) give the variable operations to be performed on the first-generation laminate to produce a second-generation design. The cutting angle (in degrees) is given first, followed by the cutting location: A, D, or AD. This designates whether the laminate is cut through the midpoints of the ascending (A), descending (D), or both (AD) legs of the design. A slash follows the letter, signifying that all the variables for making the second-generation laminate have been given.

The next number gives the cutting angle of the second-generation laminate used in making the third-generation design. The letter(s) following this number shows where to cut the laminate. This can be followed by a slash, a number, and a letter(s) and describes the procedure to be followed for making the fourth-generation laminate. The number and letter(s) have the same representation as above. Additional generations are coded in the same way.

Mitered laminate designs also can be made from materials other than wood. Chapter 11 suggests a number of applications in which these designs can be used for enhancing or decorating a variety of products. For these applications, designs are made from materials having different or contrasting colors. Here, colors are substituted for wood species in the codes for the designs. The most common colors and their letter codes are listed in Table 2. Other colors can be specified by using a combination of the codes in the table. When this system is not adequate, the actual names of the colors can be used for clarity.

These codes provide the specific procedure for making a *standard* mitered laminate or design and make it possible for anyone to duplicate a standard design made by someone else. However, there is no easy way to code the many variables for making nonstandard laminates. The procedure for making these must be, by necessity, communicated orally or with a detailed written description.

COLOR	COLOR CODE	COLOR	COLOR CODE
black	Bk	orange	O
blue	B	pink	P
brown	Br	red	R
gray	Gy	violet	V
green	G	white	W
olive	Ol	yellow	Y

Table 2. LETTER CODES FOR COLORS

Chapter 8
Simulating Mitered Laminate Designs

Although I have presented several hundred standard designs in this book, I also encourage you to experiment with nonstandard designs (see chapter 10). Indeed, there are many nonstandard procedures, patterns, and designs that await your inventiveness. There are only two fourth-generation or higher designs shown in this book, and there are only a few designs shown in which the cutting angle is other than 30°, 45° or 60°. Thus, this field is wide open for devising additional designs and patterns.

Though there are many possibilities for expanding the scope of these designs, you may wonder how you should proceed. Is it necessary to go into the shop and actually start with a linear laminate, cut cross sections, and glue them back together? Is it necessary to spend much time, materials, and energy for the sake of a new design or pattern? Do you have to be a woodworker to make mitered laminate designs?

Fortunately the answer to all these questions is no. You do not have to experiment with wood; you do not have to spend excessive time, materials, and effort; nor do you have to be a woodworker. The basic requirement is interest. Creating new designs is simple and easy and can be done by anyone sitting at a table or desk with a pencil, tracing paper, scissors, transparent tape, and some simple drawing aids available to almost anybody. Or, if you have graphics software, these designs can be made on a computer.

You cannot just draw these designs. They have to be developed via a process that is described in previous chapters. This process can be carried out either with wood, with paper and a pen, or on a computer. Only after developing the design by one of these three methods can the design then be copied onto paper.

Paper Designs

There is wide variety of tools you can use to make designs with paper (see Photo 1). You will need a way to draw parallel lines to indicate where the design is to be cut into parallel strips. To do this, place a ruler or a thin piece of wood or metal with straight and parallel sides that is the right width so that it just touches the first line drawn. Then draw a line along the other edge of the ruler. Repeat the process for the other parallel lines. The process can be simplified somewhat if you use a T-square and drawing triangles (45°/90° and 30°/60° triangles) or an adjustable angle device. Using a small, simple drawing board will make it even easier to draw these lines.

A ruler or scale is needed to determine how far apart these cutting lines should be placed. Scissors can be used to cut off the parallel strips, though straighter cuts can be made using a craft knife and a ruler or straight edge. Using a felt-tipped pen rather than a pencil to draw the stripe makes the design more pronounced. Tracing paper is not essential. Plain paper can be used if the stripe is drawn on both sides of the paper. However, the stripes must be directly opposite each other on the two sides of the paper in order for the stripe to match simultaneously on both sides of the paper.

Photo 1. AN ASSORTMENT OF SOME OF THE TOOLS YOU MAY NEED TO CREATE PAPER DESIGNS, CLOCKWISE FROM LEFT: DRAWING BOARD, T-SQUARE AND PROTRACTOR (ON DRAWING BOARD), TRANSPARENT PLASTIC TAPE, SCISSORS AND PENCIL ON TRACING PAPER, RULER, AND TRIANGLES (30°/60° AND 45°/90°)

Photo 2. THE STEPS INVOLVED IN CREATING A
FIRST-GENERATION PAPER DESIGN

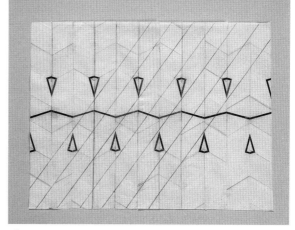

Photo 3. THE SECOND-GENERATION PAPER DESIGN
THAT HAS BEEN MARKED FOR CUTTING INTO THIRD-
GENERATION AD-SECTIONS

For the first step, cut off a piece of tracing paper about 2 inches (5 cm) wide. Draw a heavy straight line through the center of the strip (Photo 2, upper left). This represents a linear laminate with a single-strip stripe that is visible from both sides of the paper. It can be manipulated just as you would a laminate made with wood.

Next, draw diagonal lines at some angle (Photo 2, shown just under the linear laminate) across the strip of paper. All the lines must be made at the same angle with respect to the stripe and all must be the same distance apart. Lines about ½ inch (1.5 cm) apart is a practical distance. These lines designate where the piece of paper should be cut to make strips of paper.

In the third step, cut the piece of paper into strips along these parallel lines. These strips represent the cross sections. The process up to this point will have to be repeated a number of times in order to have enough of these strips to make one or more higher-generation designs. Place the cut strips side by side. Orient them so that the stripe runs upwards towards the right (ascends) in one strip and runs downward towards the right (descends) in the next strip. Alternate all the strips in this fashion. See Photo 2, lower left.

These strips of paper with the diagonal stripe are then attached to each other. Position two adjacent strips parallel to each other with contact along the edges so that the stripe in one strip lines up or matches with the stripe in the other. Simulate the gluing process with wood by connecting the two strips with transparent tape. Continue in this fashion until all the strips have been fastened together. The result is a first-generation design (Photo 2, upper right). The zigzag design should be visible from both sides of the taped design.

A first-generation design is used to make the second-generation design. In this conversion, the process is essentially the same as was described above for making the first-generation design. First, draw parallel diagonal lines at some angle across the first-generation design. Each line must go through either the center of the ascending or the center of the descending part of the design. Or it can go through the center of both. A center is that point on the design where the longitudinal centerline of a strip (equivalent to a cross section when wood is being used) intersects the stripe. It is along these lines that the design is cut in order to make strips for the next-generation design.

In the example (Photo 2, lower right), the cutting lines have been drawn through the ascending part of the design. Conventionally, cutting lines are drawn from the lower left to the upper right, but these were inadvertently drawn having the opposite, but still correct, orientation. These lines should all be the same distance apart and parallel to each other. Note that a cutting line goes through the center of every other strip or cross section. The same would be true if the lines had been drawn through the descending part of the design. Only when making an AD-design do the cutting lines go through all the cross section centers.

Cut the design (shown in Photo 2, lower right) along the dotted lines. Then repeat the procedure above for making the first-generation laminate. This will produce the second-generation design shown in Photo 3. This photo shows the cutting lines used for making the cross sections for a third-generation laminate. In this procedure, repeat the above steps. This process can be repeated, one generation at a time.

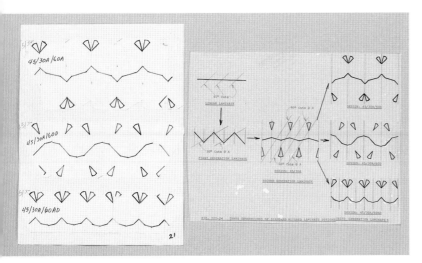

Photo 4. EXAMPLES OF MY FIRST ATTEMPTS AT CREATING DESIGNS ON PAPER

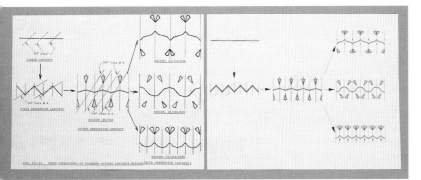

Photo 5. A HAND-DRAWN PAPER DESIGN (LEFT) AND ITS COMPUTER-GENERATED COUNTERPART

The procedure described above for making designs with paper was the first step in the process of creating all the designs in chapter 4. Initially, I made these drawings using the simple drawing tools described earlier. See Photos 4 and 5 for examples of the results of this initial procedure. After I made a design using the paper method, it was reproduced on a copier, cut out, and glued onto a sheet of paper with related designs as can be seen in Photo 4 (left). This was then reduced on a copier to the desired size. This copy, along with others that were part of the process, were used as models for copying the designs by hand onto a sheet of paper. Photo 4 (right) shows one of these hand-drawn design process sheets. (The call-outs and captions were typed on.) This was then reproduced on a copier, shown as Photo 5 (left). For comparison purposes, the photo also shows the same design as it looks when it is designed on the computer (right).

Photo 5 identifies the central figure as a second-generation 45/30A design. Also, the entire process is the same as the one used as an example for coding in chapter 7 (see page 80), except that the paper model has one rather than three strips in the stripe and the third-generation laminate is an AD-design rather than a D-design.

This process can be carried out as often as desired. It is simple, fast, and uses a small amount of material. The procedure can also be used to make and explore any number of nonstandard designs. Making paper designs like this permits you to determine beforehand what a design looks like and how the design can be altered by changing the variables. It can also be used to explore any number of nonstandard procedures by allowing you to quickly explore all facets of the process and to determine the ratio between the width and height of a design. This is a factor that is useful when making a laminate with wood that has to fit precisely into a given space. Making a design with paper or on a computer is the logical process if it is to used as a model for drawing it on paper.

Though the width of a design can be calculated from the cutting angles (described in chapter 9), simulating designs with paper (or on a computer) is the only way to calculate the height of a pattern. This also permits you to determine beforehand what a design will look like and how the design can be altered by changing the variables.

Computer Designs

Designs can also be created by anyone who has access to a computer with graphics software. Designs can be made much faster, easier, and more accurately on a computer than when using the paper/tape method. With the paper technique, it is much easier to match a single-strip stripe at the glue lines than trying to make several strips coincide. A design with a multistrip stripe is much easier to create on a computer. But, a one-strip stripe provides an accurate representation of the general shape of the design. Using a computer, the entire process can be easily carried out, from the linear laminate through any number of generations of designs.

On a computer, create a linear laminate by drawing a wide line across the computer screen. Next draw two lines at the same angle, but at an angle other than 90°, across this wide line. These two lines represent the saw cuts, and the wide line between them is the stripe. See Figure 1 (the stripe is shown in magenta). In the next step, erase (cut off or delete) the lines to the left and to the right of the angled lines. This leaves two parallel lines with the stripe running between them at an angle (Figure 2).

Next, draw a mirror image of this figure and attach the image to the original figure, as shown in Figure 3. This represents two cross sections of the first-generation design. Then create several copies of Figure 3 and connect them to each other, side by side. This results in a first-generation design as shown in Figure 4.

To generate a second-generation design, draw a pair of angled parallel lines through either two adjacent A-points or two D-points on the first-generation design. The result is shown as Figure 5. The lines represent saw cuts, and the design between the two lines represents a crosscut section from a first-generation laminate. Next erase all drawing lines except those that are between the two parallel lines. This represents the cross section from which the second-generation design will be generated. This design is developed in the same fashion as the first-generation design.

With the computer, make a mirror image of the cross section depicted in Figure 6. Join the two cross sections so that the stripes coincide as in Figure 7. Generate several of these pairs of cross sections and join them, side by side, as in Figure 8. This is a second-generation design.

This process can be repeated as often as desired, using the following steps:

1. Draw two angled, parallel lines through two central points (adjoining or alternate).

2. Erase all the drawing lines outside these two parallel lines.

3. Join the design between the two lines with its mirror image.

4. Generate and join a number of pairs of these cross sections.

This procedure will produce the next-generation of mitered laminate designs.

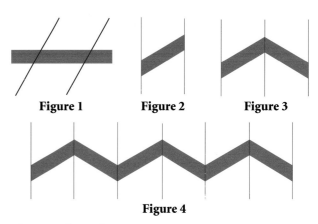

Figure 1   **Figure 2**   **Figure 3**

Figure 4

Figures 1 through 4. THE FOUR COMPUTER-GENERATED STEPS INVOLVED IN CONVERTING A LINEAR LAMINATE INTO A FIRST-GENERATION MITERED LAMINATE

Figures 5 through 8. THE FOUR COMPUTER-GENERATED STEPS INVOLVED IN CONVERTING A FIRST-GENERATION MITERED LAMINATE INTO A SECOND-GENERATION MITERED LAMINATE

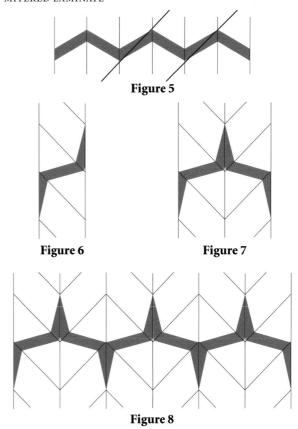

Figure 5

Figure 6   **Figure 7**

Figure 8

Chapter 9
Making Mitered Laminates Fit

This chapter describes how to make mitered laminate designs to a specific size so that they fit into a specific area. As stated in earlier chapters, the size of a mitered laminate design is directly proportional to the width of the cross sections cut from the linear laminate. The width can be calculated using procedures and equations derived in this chapter. The height of a cross section, however, is determined by modeling—making a design with paper or on a computer.

Don't let these calculations scare you. I have included them in the book to allow you to advance in the technique (beyond the projects in this book) and to give you an understanding of the relationships that exist when making mitered laminates. (This is why I have shown how I developed the equations, rather than simply giving you the final equations.)

When using mitered laminate designs for enhancing wooden items, often it is not necessary to make one that accurately fits an area. First, a design can be made to any length simply by adding more cross sections. Thus, the width of the design can normally vary over a wide range without affecting the esthetics of the decorated item. In addition, sometimes a mitered laminate is used in a project in which the size of the laminate determines the size of the item that is made. And after you have made a few items with mitered laminates, it is easy to estimate from experience how wide to cut the linear laminate cross sections for a project.

Thus, the dimensioning procedure is needed only for some projects; nonetheless, knowing how to do it can be very helpful. How to make several mitered laminate designs to a specific size is detailed in two projects in chapter 12 (pages 125 and 132). These projects illustrate the necessary steps and calculations for sizing designs.

Calculating Size

When making a mitered laminate, you must ask yourself several sizing questions. In the initial step, you will need to know how long the laminate should be. The main concern is that you have enough material to make the final design. You will also need to know how many repeating design units are needed. This is particularly important when making cylindrical objects, although it also plays a role in other design shapes. Another consideration is the height of the design. All these factors are interrelated and can be determined before beginning a project.

In mitered laminate projects in which it is important to completely fill an area with the laminate, both lengthwise and widthwise, the first step is to determine how long and how wide the design must be. The total length of the design can be achieved simply by using the required number of repeating design units. The height of a design cannot be calculated, but its ratio to the width of a repeating design unit can be determined by modelling.

To simulate a mitered laminate design, start with a stripe or the zigzag pattern on a strip of tracing paper or on the computer. The actual size is not important, as the width-to-height ratio is the same regardless of the actual size of the pattern. In the simulation, go through the same process that you would if you were using wood. Complete the design and measure the overall height of the design and the width of a repeating design unit. (A repeating design unit [RDU] is the section or part of the design that characterizes it and is repeated. In a standard laminate, it is equal to two cross sections.) Calculate the ratio of the width of a repeating design unit (W_M) to the height of the design (H_M). How this ratio (W_M/H_M) is used in calculations is detailed below. For more detailed information on formulating a repeating design unit, refer to the previous chapter on simulating mitered laminate designs with paper or a computer (page 82).

CALCULATING WIDTH AND NUMBER OF DESIGN UNITS

Having set the desired height of the design (H_D), calculate the width of a repeating design unit (W_{RDU}) as follows:

EQUATION 1

$$W_{RDU} = H_D \frac{W_M}{H_M}$$

Having established the height and width of a repeating design unit, determine the total length of laminate required for the project. This length depends on where the laminate is to be used. On a planar surface, it must reach from end to end and from top to bottom. For a circular project, the length is measured around the circumference of the design. This length must be measured along the longitudinal centerline. In this case, measure or calculate the distance around a circle that goes through the center of the design. For a planar cylindrical object, the design must reach around the periphery of the item. Having determined the total length of laminate required (L), the number of repeating design units (N_{RDU}) is calculated using Equation 2.

EQUATION 2

$$N_{RDU} = \frac{L}{W_{RDU}}$$

Most of the time, the answer will not be a whole number. A fractional part of a design unit can not normally be used in making a configured design. Only whole units can be used.

Thus, the number should be rounded off to the next even whole number. This number is then used to recalculate how wide to cut the cross sections from the linear laminate based on the total length of the design. The width and thus the height of every cross section is changed as they are inversely proportional to the number required for a specific laminate. If the original calculation was based on making the width of laminate fit exactly into a given space, then the larger number of cross sections should be chosen so that the design will not be larger than the allotted space. If the width is not that critical, the smaller number could be chosen, particularly if it is closer to the desired value. However, bear in mind that it may not be necessary to do this calculation at all if the size can vary some either way.

FACTORS AFFECTING THE SIZE OF CROSS SECTIONS

Once the width of a repeating design unit and the number of units required have been determined, the next question is how to make a repeating design unit for a specific laminate, a third-generation laminate for example, with a specified width. We have already discussed that the size of a design unit is dependent on the width of the cross sections cut from the linear laminate. Succeeding laminate cross sections are made by cutting through the design at specific points, because you do not have the option of choosing a specific width for these cross sections. Knowing the width of the final design unit, the cross sections from the linear laminate must be cut to a predetermined width. This width is determined by calculation.

There are several factors involved in converting a laminate into a design of the next generation. These factors include the change in the number of repeating design units in going from one generation to the next, the width of the repeating design unit, and the cutting angle. For accuracy, the width of the kerf removed by the saw blade must also be taken into account.

In converting any mitered laminate into a standard next-generation laminate, two repeating design units are required for each design unit of the next generation. *Thus, the number of design units required doubles every time a mitered laminate is converted.* In order to make one repeating design unit, two such units must be cut from the prior-generation laminate. This factor is included in the equations for making the calculations.

Another variable is the cutting angle. Cutting a laminate through two center points at a small angle results in a very narrow cross section that is used for making the next-generation design. A larger angle results in wider cross sections. The width of the cross section that is cut off is a direct function of the sine (abbreviated to *sin* in equations) of the cutting angle, where, in this application, the sine of the angle is the ratio of the width of a cross section cut from a laminate to the length of laminate required for the cross section.

One other factor that has an influence on the width of a cross section cut from a laminate is the loss in width of the cross section due to the saw kerf. The exact loss in width is equal to the width of the saw blade, or the kerf it cuts. This factor must be considered if accuracy is required in making a laminate for a project.

THE RELATIONSHIP BETWEEN WIDTHS OF CROSS SECTIONS

The factors that create the relationship between a laminate and the cross sections that are cut from it can be expressed mathematically. With this calculation, you can calculate how wide to cut a cross section from a linear laminate, based on the desired width of a cross section in a higher-generation laminate. To simplify the problem, all relationships, or mathematical expressions, are based on width of cross sections rather than repeating design units. It is a simple matter to convert to design units, since two cross sections are the same as one repeating design unit.

Converting a Linear Laminate

The mathematical relationship for cutting a linear laminate into cross sections is based on Figure 1.

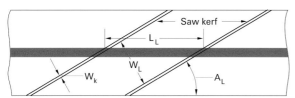

Figure 1. THE FACTORS INVOLVED IN CUTTING A LINEAR LAMINATE

The factors are:

L_L = Length of linear laminate from which a cross section is cut

W_L = Width of cross section cut from a linear laminate

W_K = Width of the saw blade kerf

A_L = Cutting angle of the linear laminate

According to the law of sines (Figure 1),

EQUATION 3

$$W_L + W_K = L_L \sin A_L$$

Rearranging this equation gives

EQUATION 4

$$L_L = \frac{(W_L + W_K)}{\sin A_L}$$

This equation is used to calculate the length of the linear laminate needed for each cross-section cut. This length times the number of cross sections needed gives the total length of linear laminate needed for the project. As shown in Figure 1, the linear laminate is cut into cross sections having the desired width (W_L).

EQUATION 5

$$^1W_L = W_L$$

This equation expresses mathematically that the width of the cross section cut from the linear laminate is the same as the width of the cross section used in making a first-generation laminate (Figure 2). The superscript on the width symbol (W) shows that this value of W is used for a specific calculation. A one (1) means that this equation is used for determining how wide to cut cross sections from a linear laminate when making a first-generation laminate; a two (2) shows that the equation is used when making a second-generation laminate; a three (3) shows that the equation is used when making a third-generation laminate, and so forth.

As I have already discussed, in deriving equivalent equations that are used for higher generation laminates, the loss of material due to the saw kerf has to be considered. Though small, the loss reduces the width of cross sections cut from the laminate. The calculations are much simpler and easier if this loss is ignored, but the errors produced are large. To illustrate this error, the equations are developed for both situations (see Table 1 on page 92). In the first derivations, the saw kerf loss is ignored. These equations give only approximate solutions. In the approximate equations, the equal symbol (=) has been replaced by the "approximately equals" symbol (≈). The loss due to the saw kerf is accounted for in the exact equations. After developing the equations for both methods, the two are compared and the errors resulting from using the approximate method are given. Equation 5 does not involve the width of the saw kerf, so it is the same for both the approximate and the exact method.

Converting a First-Generation Laminate

In making a second-generation laminate in which the cross sections have to be a specific width, you must determine how wide the cross sections must be that are cut from the linear laminate. Both the approximate and the exact equations are derived below; the factors involved are shown in Figure 2.

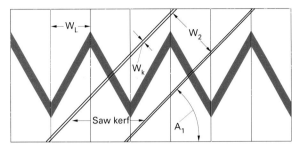

Figure 2. THE FACTORS INVOLVED IN CUTTING A FIRST-GENERATION LAMINATE

The factors are:

W_L = Width of cross sections cut from the linear laminate

W_2 = Width of cross sections cut for the second-generation laminate

W_K = Width of the saw blade kerf

A_1 = Cutting angle for the first-generation laminate

The approximate mathematical relationship between the above factors is expressed as follows:

EQUATION 6

$$W_2 \approx 2W_L \sin A_1$$

Solving the equation for W_L but replacing W_L by ^2W_L because this is the equation that specifically applies to the width of a linear cross section needed for a second-generation laminate gives

EQUATION 7

$$^2W_L \approx \frac{W_2}{2 \sin A_1}$$

Equation 8 calculates the exact relationship in which the loss due to the width of the saw kerf (W_K) is included:

EQUATION 8

$$^2W_L = \frac{(W_2 + W_K)}{2 \sin A_1}$$

Fill in the values for the desired width of the cross sections for the second-generation laminate (W_2), the width of the saw kerf (W_K), and the cutting angle (A_1) into the above equation, then solve the equation. The answer is the required width of the cross sections to be cut from the linear laminate.

Note that the derivation of the equations for the exact method are not shown, only the final equation. The steps for developing the final equation in each case is the same as those given for the approximate method with one difference. The width of cross sections includes the loss due to the saw kerf where (W) is replaced by (W + W_K) in the derivation.

Converting a Second-Generation Laminate

Figure 3 shows the factors involved when a third-generation laminate is made.

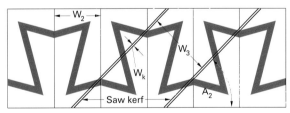

Figure 3. THE FACTORS INVOLVED IN CUTTING A SECOND-GENERATION LAMINATE

The factors are:

W_2 = Width of cross sections cut from the first-generation laminate

W_3 = Width of cross sections cut for a third-generation laminate

W_K = Width of the saw blade kerf

A_2 = Cutting angle for the second-generation laminate

The approximate mathematical relationships between the three factors above are similar to those for the prior generation and are expressed as follows:

EQUATION 9

$$W_3 \approx 2W_2 \sin A_2$$

Rearranging gives

EQUATION 10

$$W_2 \approx \frac{W_3}{2 \sin A_2}$$

Substituting this value of W_2 into Equation 7 gives

EQUATION 11

$${}^3W_L \approx \frac{\dfrac{W_3}{2 \sin A_2}}{2 \sin A_1}$$

Note that the superscript on the W_L has been changed from a 2 to a 3 to reflect an equation for a third-generation laminate. Simplifying gives

EQUATION 12

$${}^3W_L \approx \frac{W_3}{(2 \sin A_1)(2 \sin A_2)}$$

The equivalent exact equation when the width of the saw blade kerf is taken into account is as follows:

EQUATION 13

$${}^3W_L = \frac{W_3 + W_K(1 + 2 \sin A_2)}{(2 \sin A_1)(2 \sin A_2)}$$

The exact equation (Equation 13) is the same as the approximate equation (Equation 12), except the width has been corrected for the loss due to the saw blade kerf. The solution to Equation 13 gives the exact width of cross sections to be cut from the linear laminate (${}^3W_L$) when the desired width of a third-generation cross section is W_3. For an example of how this equation is used, see page 93.

Converting a Third-Generation Laminate

Figure 4 shows the factors involved when making a fourth-generation laminate.

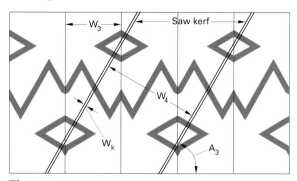

Figure 4. THE FACTORS INVOLVED IN CUTTING A THIRD-GENERATION LAMINATE

The factors are:

W_3 = Width of cross section cut from the second-generation laminate

W_4 = Width of cross section cut for a fourth-generation laminate

W_K = Width of the saw blade kerf

A_3 = Cutting angle of the third-generation laminate

The approximate relationship from Figure 4 is as follows:

EQUATION 14

$$W_4 \approx 2W_3 \sin A_3$$

Rearranging gives

EQUATION 15

$$W_3 \approx \frac{W_4}{2 \sin A_3}$$

Substituting the value of W_3 into Equation 12 (where the superscript on the W_L has been changed to a four [4] to reflect the application of the equation to a fourth-generation laminate) gives

EQUATION 16

$${}^4W_L \approx \frac{\dfrac{W_4}{2 \sin A_3}}{(2 \sin A_1)(2 \sin A_2)}$$

Simplifying gives

EQUATION 17

$$^4W_L \approx \frac{W_4}{(2\sin A_1)\,(2\sin A_2)\,(2\sin A_3)}$$

Correcting for the width of the saw kerf, the exact equivalent to Equation 17 is

EQUATION 18

$$^4W_L = \frac{W_4 + W_K\,[1 + 2\sin A_3 + (2\sin A_2)(2\sin A_3)]}{(2\sin A_1)\,(2\sin A_2)\,(2\sin A_3)}$$

The solution of Equation 18 gives the exact width of the linear laminate cross sections needed for making a fourth-generation laminate of width W_4.

Converting a Fourth-Generation Laminate

Figure 5 shows the factors involved in converting a fourth-generation to a fifth-generation laminate.

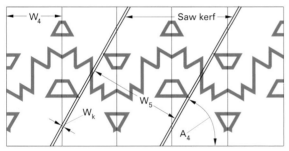

Figure 5. THE FACTORS INVOLVED IN CUTTING A FOURTH-GENERATION LAMINATE

The factors are:

W_4 = Width of cross sections cut from the third-generation laminate

W_5 = Width of cross sections cut for a fifth-generation laminate

W_K = Width of the saw blade kerf

A_4 = Cutting angle of the fourth-generation laminate

As before, the approximate relationship is as follows:

EQUATION 19

$$W_5 \approx 2W_4 \sin A_4$$

Rearranging gives

EQUATION 20

$$W_4 \approx \frac{W_5}{2\sin A_4}$$

Substituting this value of W_4 into Equation 17 (changing the superscript on the W_L to a 5) gives

EQUATION 21

$$^5W_L \approx \frac{\dfrac{W_5}{2\sin A_4}}{(2\sin A_1)\,(2\sin A_2)\,(2\sin A_3)}$$

Simplifying gives

EQUATION 22

$$^5W_L \approx \frac{W_5}{(2\sin A_1)\,(2\sin A_2)\,(2\sin A_3)\,(2\sin A_4)}$$

The exact relationship comparable to Equation 22 is

EQUATION 23

$$^5W_L = \frac{W_5 + W_K\,[1 + 2\sin A_4 + (2\sin A_3)(2\sin A_4) + (2\sin A_2)(2\sin A_3)(2\sin A_4)]}{(2\sin A_1)\,(2\sin A_2)\,(2\sin A_3)\,(2\sin A_4)}$$

The solution to Equation 23 gives the exact width of linear laminate cross sections required (^5W_L) to make a fifth-generation laminate, having cross sections with a width of W_5. If needed, equations for higher-generation laminates can be derived in a similar manner.

Error from Use of
Approximate Calculation Method

The error in using the simple approximate formulas is rather large—especially for higher-generation laminates. In Table 1, values for the two methods are calculated and compared. The values are calculated for the first five generations of laminates where all the cutting angles are either 30° or 60°. In the calculation, the saw kerf was assumed to be ⅛ inch (3 mm) wide. The values in the table give the width of cross sections that have to be cut from a linear laminate so the sections in the respective final laminate will have a width of 1 inch (2.5 cm).

TYPE OF STANDARD MITERED LAMINATE	30° CUTTING ANGLE			60° CUTTING ANGLE		
	APPROX. METHOD	EXACT METHOD	% ERROR	APPROX. METHOD	EXACT METHOD	% ERROR
First Generation	1.000	1.000	0	1.000	1.000	0
Second Generation	1.000	1.125	-11.1	0.577	0.650	-11.2
Third Generation	1.000	1.250	-20.0	0.333	0.447	-25.5
Fourth Generation	1.000	1.375	-27.3	0.192	0.330	-42.8
Fifth Generation	1.000	1.500	-33.3	0.111	0.263	-57.8

Table 1. COMPARISON OF APPROXIMATE AND EXACT METHODS FOR CALCULATING WIDTH OF CROSS-SECTIONS REQUIRED

The errors are based on the difference between the exact method and the approximate method. Though the exact method is more difficult to calculate, it becomes necessary if the finished laminate has to be made up of a specified number of cross sections (or repeating design units) to fit a select space.

The sine of angles can be obtained from a scientific calculator or from a table of trigonometric functions. The sines of a few common angles are given in Table 2.

DEGREE OF ANGLE	SINE OF ANGLE
15	0.2588
30	0.5000
45	0.7071
60	0.8660
75	0.9659

Table 2. SINE OF COMMON ANGLES

Sample Calculations

The following example demonstrates the calculations that must be made to determine how wide to cut the initial cross sections from a linear laminate. *Note*: If you are using metric measurements, all relationships will be the same. The example is based on the following premises:

1. Desired height of design—1½ inches
2. Chosen laminate design—(3/16C)(1/8M)2 1/2W (23/32)45/30A/75D
3. Length of design—to encircle an 8-inch-diameter vase
4. Width of the saw kerf— ⅛ inch

The chosen design is the same as the one used in the example in chapter 7 as well as the one used in making the square cutting board (right) shown on page 19. In this example, dimensioning is based on the drawing made of the design in which the numbers are proportional to the actual widths in the wood model. Also for the drawing, colors were used instead of wood species.

In the first step, using the paper method or a computer, draw the third-generation design to determine the width-to-height ratio (W_M/H_M) of a repeating design unit. Based on this drawing (Figure 6), this ratio is one

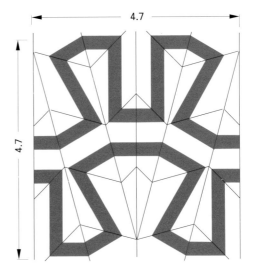

Figure 6. REPEATING DESIGN UNIT FOR A 45/30A/75D MITERED LAMINATE

(4.7/4.7 = 1, obtained by measuring the width and height of the design on the drawing). Using this ratio, calculate the width of a repeating design unit (W_{RDU}) according to Equation 1 on page 87. Having set the design height (H_D) at 1½ inches, the repeating design unit would also be 1½ inches wide, since the width-to-height ratio is one.

Next, calculate the total length of design (L) needed. It is equal to the diameter of the vase times pi, or 8 inches x 3.1416 = 25.133 inches, which is about 25⅛ inches.

Using these two values, calculate the total number of repeating design units (N_{RDU}) required for the project, using Equation 2 on page 87.

$$N_{RDU} = L/W_{RDU} = (25⅛")/(1½") = 16¾$$

Since this should be a whole number divisible by 2, select 16 as the number of repeating design units to use in the project. Then recalculate the width of each using 16 as the number. For a design 25⅛ inches long, the width of a repeating design unit then becomes:

$$(25⅛")/(16) = 1.570" \text{ or approximately } 1\tfrac{9}{16}"$$

In the calculations to follow, it is simpler to use the width of a cross section rather than repeating design units. One repeating design unit has the same width as two cross sections. The third-generation cross section width is thus half the width of a repeating design unit or 25/32 inch (0.781 inch).

Use Equation 13 on page 90 to calculate how wide to cut the cross sections from the linear laminate so that the sections in the chosen design have a width of 25/32 inch. In this equation,

W_3 = 25/32" or 0.781"

W_K = ⅛" or 0.125"

$\sin A_1 = \sin 45° = 0.707$

$\sin A_2 = \sin 60° = 0.866$

According to Equation 13 (see page 90),

$^3W_L = [W_3 + W_K(1 + 2\sin A_2)]/[(2\sin A_1)(2\sin A_2)]$

$= [0.781 + 0.125[1+(2)(0.866)]/[(2)(0.707)(2)(0.866)]$

$= [0.781 + (0.125)(2.732)]/[(1.414)(1.732)]$

$= (0.781 + 0.3415)/2.449 = 1.1265/2.449 = 0.4584$

$= \text{approximately } 15/32"$

Based on the above calculation, cutting the linear laminate cross sections 15/32 inch wide will produce third-generation sections that are 25/32 inch wide.

If the approximate method had been used to calculate the width of cross sections required to make this third-generation laminate, the results would be as follows using Equation 12 (see page 90):

$^3W_L \approx W_3/(2\sin A_1)(2\sin A_2)$

$\approx 0.781/(2)(\sin 45°)(2)(\sin 60°)$

$\approx 0.781/(2)(0.707)(2)(0.866)$

$\approx 0.781/2.449 = 0.3189$

$\approx \text{approximately } 5/16"$

This compares to 15/32", which was calculated by the exact method. In this example, the error is

$[(5/16" - 15/32")/(15/32")]100 = -33.3\% \text{ error}$

The other information needed for the project is how long the linear laminate needs to be for the third-generation laminate to encircle an 8-inch-diameter vase. The total length needed is based on the length of linear laminate required for each third-generation cross section. This calculation is based on Equation 4 (see page 88).

$L_L = (W_L + W_K)/\sin A_L$

$= (15/32" + ⅛")/\sin 30°$

$= (15/32" + 4/32")/0.500$

$= (19/32")/0.500 = 19/16" \text{ or } 1\tfrac{3}{16}"$

For 32 sections (equal to 16 repeating design units) each requiring a 1 3/16-inch length of linear laminate, it requires

$32 \times 1\tfrac{3}{16}" = 38" \text{ of linear laminate}$

This is the total length required for the actual design. In making the design, however, there are some losses or waste, in addition to the saw kerf. Each time a laminate is cut into cross sections, the ends of the laminate cannot be converted to sections and are wasted. Also some error may be made in cutting cross sections that cannot be used. A good rule is to allow about 10% loss for each conversion from one laminate to the next generation. In this case, three conversions would result in about a 30% loss. Thus, make the linear laminate 30% longer than calculated or about 50 inches (127 cm) long.

Chapter 10
Nonstandard Procedures and Designs

The emphasis of this book has been the many facets of characterizing and defining standard procedures and standard mitered laminates. A deviation from just one step of the procedure produces a *nonstandard* laminate. This chapter explores the types of laminates or designs that are obtained if only one, or perhaps two, variables in the process are nonstandard. The type of designs that are obtained if you add a step or two at the end of the standard process is also discussed. Combining two or more variations when making a laminate also opens the door to many possible nonstandard designs. You will find that the variations described in this chapter suggest others, which will lead to many nonstandard laminates and designs.

I will also discuss deviations from the standard procedure in making cross sections from a linear laminate. This includes cutting the sections at more than one angle or at more than one width. There is also a sampling of the designs produced if none of the cross sections are turned over before gluing.

An overview of nonstandard designs would not be complete without designs created with laminates other than linear mitered laminates. A laminate does not have to be cut at every central point. It can be cut at any other point. Another option is to alternate between cutting a point and skipping the next point. The design can also be cut through points other than the A-points or D-points. The final variation discussed in this chapter is the addition of a nonstandard step (or two) to the procedure.

Nonstandard Linear Laminates

Only a small sampling of the many possible variations in nonstandard linear laminates are described here. The vase shown in Photo 1 exhibits examples of nonstandard design. In this example, six different designs encircle the periphery of the vase.

A few of the designs made by the mitered laminate process in this book are similar to ones in written material I've found. Some of the laminates I've seen are photos of items on exhibit in galleries or showrooms—with no description of how they were made. The other laminates I've seen, with one exception, have only designs that look like first-generation laminates.

Of all the mitered laminated processes I have seen in published material, making flat, planar items with *chevron* designs (or V-shaped designs—what I call a

Photo 1. A VASE MADE WITH SIX NONSTANDARD MITERED LAMINATE DESIGNS; 9 X 11½ INCHES (23 X 29 CM); WALNUT AND ABOUT EIGHT UNKNOWN WOOD SPECIES

zigzag pattern in this book) is the only example of using the process that I describe in this book; making a chevron is the same as making a first-generation design. Though I did not find a reference to a second-generation design made by the mitered laminate process in the material, it was my nephew's example that inspired me to develop the mitered laminate process in this book. All the other laminates that were described in the material I read were made by the segmenting method. This method is briefly described in chapter 1 (see Photos 5 through 8 in that chapter).

For your reference, I have listed the material that I found in a survey of the published information in the field. The following articles contain designs similar to the ones that can be made by the mitered laminate process, though they take the process only as far as the first generation.

In the October 1990 issue of *American Woodworker* (No. 16, p. 78), a gallery photo shows a lidded vessel made by James A. Neff, Jr. with a zigzag (first-generation) five-strip stripe. This design is similar to the design on the vase shown in Photo 1, chapter 2 (page 17). In this photo, it may be difficult to see all five stripes, since it was made up of one wide strip of walnut and four strips of veneer.

Woodturning magazine, in the spring of 1991 (No. 3, p. 47), featured vessels made by George Radeschi. These were made by using segmented rings (briefly described in chapter 1, page 12). Several vessels with the zigzag pattern (similar to the vase in Photo 1, chapter 2), three with square diamond designs (similar to Figure 30, Pattern Q in this chapter), and one with a regular diamond design (similar to Figure 30, Pattern R in this chapter) are shown.

An earlier article in *Woodwork* (Winter 1989, No. 4, p. 69) showed a gallery photo of another George Radeschi vessel with a zigzag design, but made no mention of how it was made. It was probably made in the same way as described in the *Woodturning* article above. In the same issue, a gallery photo of Richard David Julian's vessel made with a zigzag design was shown.

This method of making vessels with segmented rings (see chapter 1, page 12) is described by Addie Draper and Bud Latven in the September/October 1985 issue of *Fine Woodworking* (No. 54, p. 6). One vessel featured a zigzag design and another one a design as shown in Figure 31, Pattern U in this chapter. These designs can also be made using the mitered laminate process (see center

design in Photo 1 in this chapter). Another vessel made by the segmented-ring method is shown in the April 1987 issue of *Fine Woodworking* (No. 63, p. 118). It was made by Burrell A. Fletcher and also features a zigzag pattern.

Last, a book by Emmett E. Brown and Cyril Brown called *Polychromatic Assembly for Woodturning* (Linden Publishing Co., 1982) describes several items made with designs made using the first step in the mitered laminate process. The planar items with linear zigzag designs (what they call chevrons) were made using the mitered laminate process to make these first-generation designs. Turned vessels were made by the segmented ring method. Plate 52, page 95, shows a vessel with a peripheral pattern that is the same as a second-generation 45/45D laminate (same as the design on the left in Figure 30, Pattern S in this chapter and in Photo 13, chapter 1).

Other than planar chevron, first-generation designs, I have been unable to find a single example of designs made by using the mitered laminate process. However, I should mention that some bandings are made by a process that has some steps that are similar to the mitered laminate process. Bandings ($\frac{1}{16}$ inch to 1 inch or 2 mm to 2.5 cm wide) are strips of laminated wood with designs. They are inlaid and glued into grooves or dadoes cut into flat furniture tops, drawer fronts, chair backs, and so forth as decorative borders. In this process, some of the bandings are made by gluing strips of different woods together. The laminate is then cut into cross sections, and these are then reassembled in a different configuration. For more complex designs, the process can be repeated. The product is a narrow strip of laminated woods with small repeating geometrical patterns along its length. Though the process has some similarities to the mitered laminate process, the products are very different and are used for different purposes.

NONLAMINATED BOARD

Previous chapters discussed how to use a standard linear laminate, a standard stripe sandwiched between two boards of the same species or color, as the starting material. However, it is not necessary to start with a standard laminate. One deviation from a standard linear laminate is to simply use a board—one with no laminated stripe—to make a mitered laminate. Other than starting with a nonstandard linear laminate, the process is the same as for making a standard laminate.

In this method, the change in direction of the wood grain results in interesting and artistic designs and patterns.

This process is shown in four illustrations (Figures 1 through 4). Note that, in these illustrations, all the glue lines are shown; the cross sections are assembled and glued, but the mitered ends are not trimmed. First, cut a board into cross sections at 60° (Figure 1), reassemble the sections, then glue them together to form a first-generation laminate (Figure 2), following all standard procedures. Then cut this laminate at 45° into cross sections through the A-points and reconstruct the sections into a second-generation laminate as depicted in Figure 3. If the cut is made through D-points, the design of the second-generation laminate will be different. Figure 4 shows the results when the laminate in Figure 3 is converted into a third-generation laminate by making a 60° cut through the D-points.

The final result is a 60/45A/60D laminate design. The design is created by the wood grain running in different directions in the small mitered pieces. These designs are the same as ones made with a standard laminate, except that they do not have a stripe. In the case of a standard design, however, it is often difficult to see any design other than the one made by the stripe.

TWO LAMINATED WOOD SPECIES

Another variation on using a standard linear laminate is to use two boards of different species, color, or grain that are glued or laminated together without a stripe. Thus, the contrast between the two boards provides the design.

This process is the same as the one described for the standard laminate (see chapter 2), except that there are two ways to glue the cross sections together and each procedure produces a different design. In the first one, cross sections are turned end over end then glued together. In the other, the sections are turned edge over edge. This produces twice as many designs as the standard procedure. (The sections can also be turned over in the two ways described above when making standard laminates. In this case, however, the same design is produced by either alternative.)

Converting the initial laminate made from the two contrasting boards into first-generation laminates is demonstrated in Figure 5. In this illustration, one wood species is depicted in magenta and the other species in white. Cut the linear laminate into cross sections at 45°.

Figure 1. A BOARD MARKED FOR CUTTING INTO CROSS SECTIONS

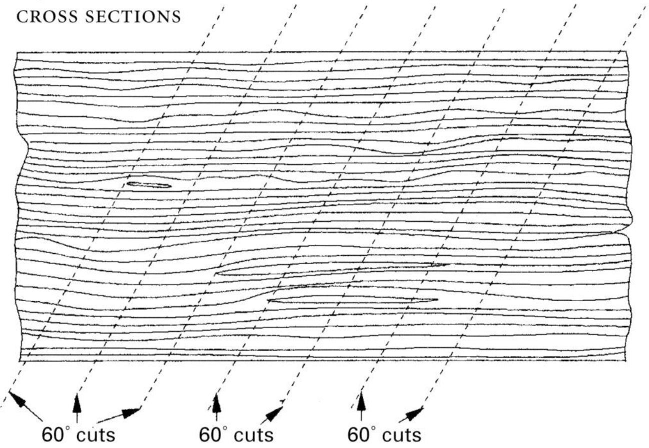

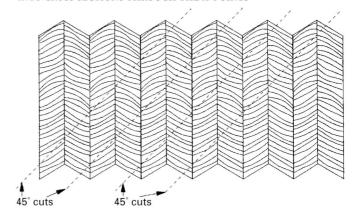

Figure 2. FIRST-GENERATION LAMINATE MADE FROM THE BOARD SECTIONS IN FIGURE 1, MARKED FOR CUTTING INTO CROSS SECTIONS THROUGH THE A-POINTS

Figure 3. SECOND-GENERATION LAMINATE MADE FROM THE SECTIONS CUT FROM THE FIRST-GENERATION LAMINATE IN FIGURE 2 AND MARKED FOR CUTTING INTO CROSS SECTIONS THROUGH THE D-POINTS

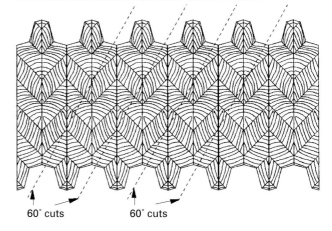

Figure 4. THIRD-GENERATION LAMINATE MADE FROM SECTIONS FROM THE SECOND-GENERATION LAMINATE IN FIGURE 3

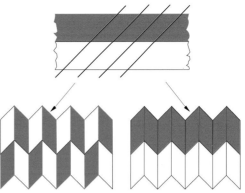

Figure 5. THE TWO FIRST-GENERATION DESIGNS PRODUCED FROM A LINEAR LAMINATE COMPOSED OF TWO WOOD SPECIES WITHOUT A STRIPE

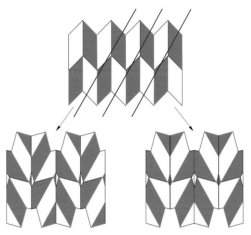

Figure 6. THE TWO SECOND-GENERATION A-DESIGNS PRODUCED FROM THE SAME FIRST-GENERATION MITERED LAMINATE IN FIGURE 5, LEFT

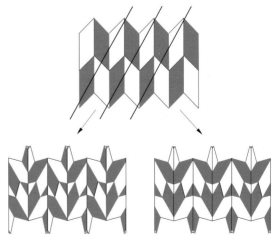

Figure 7. THE TWO SECOND-GENERATION D-DESIGNS PRODUCED FROM THE SAME FIRST-GENERATION MITERED LAMINATE IN FIGURE 5, LEFT

For the first-generation pattern on the left, alternate cross sections from the linear laminate are turned end over end, then glued. In this checkerboard pattern, each wood species alternates and is in either the top half of the design or the bottom half.

When the sections are turned edge over edge, the pattern obtained is shown on the right in Figure 5. Here, each wood species produces a zigzag pattern, the same as a standard linear laminate that has been converted to a first-generation laminate. In this conversion, one wood species is located along the upper half of the design, and the other is on the lower half.

To make second-generation laminates, cut the first-generation laminates into sections. Cut the laminate with the checkerboard design through the A-points, assemble the sections, and glue them together. The resulting designs are shown in Figure 6. Turn alternate sections end over end to get the pattern shown in the lower left. When the sections are turned edge over edge, the pattern in the lower right results.

Cutting the checkerboard design through the D-points results in two different second-generation D-laminates. The process is illustrated in Figure 7. The design in the lower left is created when the sections are turned end over end. Turn the cross sections edge over edge to achieve the pattern in the lower right.

Convert the first-generation laminate with the zig-zag design (see Figure 5, lower right) into two second-generation designs as described above for the checkerboard laminate. The patterns resulting from cutting through the A-points are depicted in Figure 8. The design on the left results when the sections are turned end over end. The edge-over-edge process gives the patterns on the right.

As above, two other designs are created when the cuts are made through the D-center points. Turning the sections end over end results in the pattern on the left in Figure 9. At the right is the design resulting when the sections are turned edge over edge. Thus, one linear laminate produces eight second-generation designs at every cutting angle.

All eight second-generation designs shown in the above figures exhibit symmetry along the glue lines in different ways. Some generalizations can be made about these designs. Observe the four in which the cross sections are turned edge over edge. The pattern on one side of every glue line (the last one) is a mirror image of the other side. These are the designs shown in the lower right corner of Figures 6 through 9. In the other four designs, this glue line normally reflects the other species of wood. These are the lower left designs in the same four figures. In the designs on the left in Figures 6 and 7, every mitered block of one species is adjacent only to the other species of wood. This results when the cross sections from both the linear and the first-generation laminate are turned end over end.

TWO LAMINATED WOOD SPECIES WITH A STRIPE

Intriguing and complex designs are also possible when the linear laminate is made up of a standard stripe sandwiched between two woods of different species. The contrast in color, texture, or grain between the two outboard planks and the stripe makes the design interesting.

Two general variations are possible here: one in which two outboard planks are different (nonstandard), while the remainder of the process follows the standard procedure; the other also uses two different outboard planks, but the procedure for assembling and gluing the cross sections together is nonstandard.

When the standard procedure is followed, a laminate is changed into two different designs at every standard

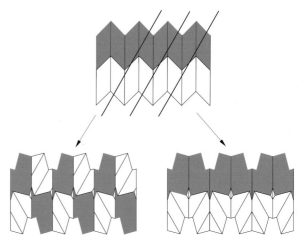

Figure 8. THE TWO SECOND-GENERATION A-DESIGNS PRODUCED FROM THE SAME FIRST-GENERATION MITERED LAMINATE IN FIGURE 5, RIGHT

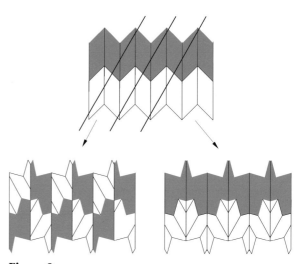

Figure 9. THE TWO SECOND-GENERATION D-DESIGNS PRODUCED FROM THE SAME FIRST-GENERATION MITERED LAMINATE IN FIGURE 5, RIGHT

conversion and many designs are possible. Except for the stripe itself, most designs made from this nonstandard linear laminate result in patterns that are unconnected or are noncontinuous. There are, however, a few variations in which the two species of wood, as well as the stripe, form connected designs or patterns. The result is a mitered laminate that has at least three connected designs. The stripe forms one design; the other designs are formed from the two species of wood. The type of design obtained depends on the way the cross sections are turned over when going from one generation to the next.

Next, I'll describe the process of making laminates that have more than one connected design feature. To show the different designs, the normal stripe is shown as a broad, black line. The two species of wood used as outboard planks are shown in magenta and white. Except for using a nonstandard linear laminate, the rest of the process follows the standard procedure. Extra precaution must be taken to orient the cross sections at every conversion to get these connected designs. Most orientations produce interesting designs, as was shown in the illustrations for the second alternative above (pages 97 and 98). The purpose here, however, is to create designs that match and are continuous at the glue lines. This type of design represents only a small percentage of the total number possible.

In the series of mitered laminates produced in the process of making this 60/45A/45D/60D design (Figures 10 through 14), the way the cross sections are turned over in each conversion is specified. In the figures, all of the glue lines, or the surfaces that had been cut and glued together, are shown as light black lines. The black dotted lines indicate the locations where the laminate is cut when making sections for the next-generation laminate. In this series of drawings, the sharp points on the converted laminate have been cut off to produce straight edges.

To make the designs shown in the following figures, begin with a linear laminate consisting of a stripe flanked on one side by a light-colored wood and on the other side by a darker species of wood. Use a standard method for assembling cross sections. Cut the laminate into cross sections at 60° (Figure 10). Turn alternate sections end over end and glue these together. This first-generation laminate (Figure 11) exhibits the checkerboard design. Saw this laminate into sections at 45° through the A-points. Turn alternate sections edge over edge and glue together into a second-generation design as shown in Figure 12. In addition to the continuous design formed by the stripe (shown as a broad black line), both wood species have connected zigzag patterns. While the stripe is a 60/45A design, each of the two outboard planks produces a 45 pattern.

Figure 13 shows the pattern produced when the 60/45A laminate is converted into a third-generation laminate by the following procedure: Saw sections at 45° through the D-points and turn alternate sections edge

Figure 10. LINEAR LAMINATE WITH A STRIPE BUT DIFFERENT OUTBOARD PLANKS CUT AT 60° FOR A FIRST-GENERATION DESIGN

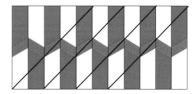

Figure 11. FIRST-GENERATION LAMINATE DESIGN NO. 60 CUT AT 45° THROUGH THE A-POINTS FOR A SECOND-GENERATION LAMINATE

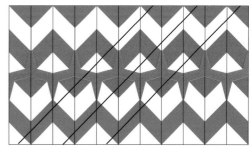

Figure 12. SECOND-GENERATION LAMINATE WITH STRIPE DESIGN NO. 60/45A CUT AT 45° THROUGH THE D-POINTS FOR A THIRD-GENERATION LAMINATE

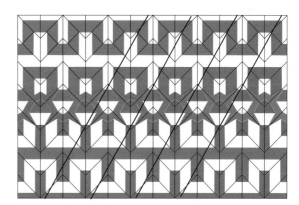

Figure 13. THIRD-GENERATION LAMINATE WITH STRIPE DESIGN NO. 60/45A/45D CUT AT 60° THROUGH THE D-POINTS FOR A FOURTH-GENERATION LAMINATE

over edge. Notice that, with each conversion, the design has become more complex. This third-generation laminate (60/45A/45D) exhibits three distinct connected designs. The up-across-down-across pattern (45/45D pattern) is produced by both wood species. The other pattern that results from each of these species is a 45/45A design. These designs are repeated if the initial linear laminate is made with wider outboard planks.

Convert this third-generation laminate into the next generation by cutting it into sections at 60° through the D-points. Turn the cross sections edge over edge to make the design (60/45A/45D/60D) in Figure 14. In addition to the broad black stripe, more than one continuous or connected design is produced by each wood species. The actual number depends on the width of the linear laminate. These are not standard laminate designs. However, small sections of the designs are similar to standard ones presented in prior chapters.

Only one series of examples was presented to illustrate this technique, but it has wide applicability. For every standard first-, second-, third-, or fourth-generation design, there are several possible designs that can be made from a linear laminate with different outboard planks. The total number is geometric with respect to the generation of the laminate. A linear laminate converts into two first-generation designs. Each of these produces four second-generation laminates, for a total of eight from the two laminates. These eight can then be converted into 32 third-generation designs. In turn, 128 fourth-generation laminates can be made from these 32.

This is an area in which much original work can be done exploring the many design variations.

The other variation is the use of two different species of wood as the outboard planks and a standard stripe, but using a nonstandard procedure for assembling the cross sections. In all cases, the stripe is matched, going from one cross section to the adjacent ones, but other parts of the design may not match. This can yield many more designs than using a completely standard process. Only a sampling of the many variations possible is illustrated with second- and third-generation designs. Figures 15 through 17 illustrate second-generation designs made by this variation of the process. Figures 18 through 25 are third-generation designs.

A design with a single-strip stripe (black) is shown in Figure 19. A five-strip stripe is illustrated in Figures 22 and 25, where black, magenta, and pink make up the stripe. The rest of the figures show three-strip stripes, using black and another color. The outboard planks are represented by white and another color.

An additional nonstandard linear laminate is one in which only the stripe is nonstandard. (The stripe is discussed in chapters 3 and 5.) A nonstandard stripe is typically made up of two or more strips of different species of wood arranged in any order, but not symmetrically. Because the stripes do not match when turned over, they cannot be arranged to form a connected or continuous stripe. They must be offset at the glue line. This type of design is discussed in more detail in the latter part of this chapter.

Figure 14. FOURTH-GENERATION LAMINATE WITH STRIPE DESIGN NO. 60/45A/45D/60D

Figure 15. A NONSTANDARD SECOND-GENERATION DESIGN WITH A THREE-STRIP STRIPE

Figure 16. A NONSTANDARD SECOND-GENERATION
DESIGN WITH A THREE-STRIP STRIPE

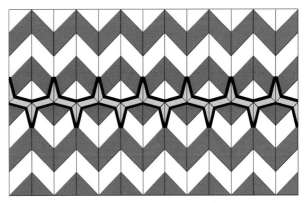

Figure 17. A NONSTANDARD SECOND-GENERATION
DESIGN WITH A THREE-STRIP STRIPE

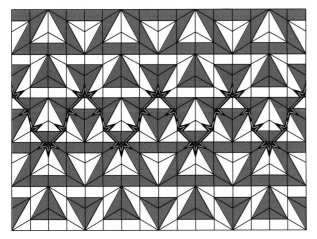

Figure 18. A NONSTANDARD THIRD-GENERATION DESIGN
WITH A THREE-STRIP STRIPE

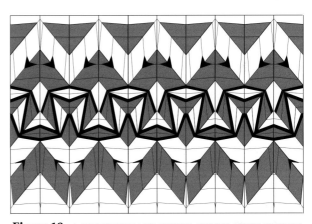

Figure 19. A NONSTANDARD THIRD-GENERATION DESIGN
WITH A ONE-STRIP STRIPE

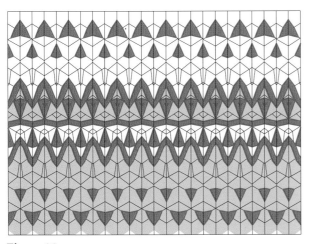

Figure 20. A NONSTANDARD THIRD-GENERATION DESIGN
WITH A THREE-STRIP STRIPE

Figure 21. A NONSTANDARD THIRD-GENERATION DESIGN
WITH A THREE-STRIP STRIPE

Figure 22. A NONSTANDARD THIRD-GENERATION DESIGN WITH A FIVE-STRIP STRIPE

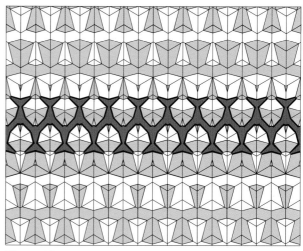

Figure 23. A NONSTANDARD THIRD-GENERATION DESIGN WITH A THREE-STRIP STRIPE

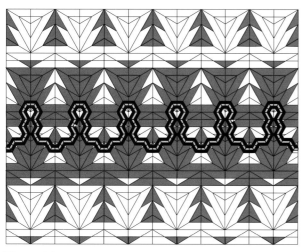

Figure 24. A NONSTANDARD THIRD-GENERATION DESIGN WITH A THREE-STRIP STRIPE

Figure 25. A NONSTANDARD THIRD-GENERATION DESIGN WITH A FIVE-STRIP STRIPE

Photo 2. BOWL MADE BY THE SEGMENTED RING METHOD; 9 X 4 INCHES (23 X 10 CM)

Photo 3. CHEESE BOARD MADE FROM LINEAR LAMINATE; $10\frac{1}{2}$ X $7\frac{3}{4}$ X $\frac{7}{8}$ INCH (27 X 20 X 2.2 CM)

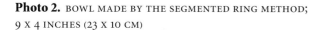

Cross Sections

Another variable in the process is the cutting of crosscut sections. In the standard procedure, a linear laminate is cut into sections at one angle, all at the same width. A generation laminate is cut through either or both of its center points. Varying either of these variables produces a nonstandard laminate. In addition, different nonstandard designs are created if the cross sections are not glued together in the standard manner. One variation is not matching the stripe at the glue lines. Another is not turning over any of the sections before the gluing process. How all of these variables affect the final pattern is discussed below. In each figure, only the stripe (heavy magenta line) and the glue lines are shown. Where applicable, the cutting line is represented by a heavier black line.

VARIABLE ANGLES

The second step in the standard procedure is cutting the linear laminate at a constant angle into cross sections of equal width. If all cuts are not made at the same angle, but all of the other standard procedures are followed, the normal zigzag pattern is not produced. Such a non-standard design is shown as Pattern A in Figure 26. The pattern has no symmetry or direction, nor does it repeat itself. Note that the angle in the design is double the size of the cutting angle.

VARIABLE WIDTHS

An irregular zigzag pattern with no symmetry is produced if the width of each cross section is varied (but cut at a constant angle), assembled, and glued in the standard fashion (see Pattern B, Figure 26). Cut a linear laminate at a constant angle into cross sections of two different widths. Glue these together alternately; that is, one narrow section, then one wide section, followed by one narrow section, and so forth. This produces a design with a longitudinal axis that is not at right angles to its transverse axis (shown as Pattern C, Figure 26).

An alternative method is to glue two narrow sections together, join these to a pair of wide sections, then bond them to two narrow sections, and so forth. The design is different from a normal zigzag pattern (see Pattern D, Figure 26). It is symmetrical and its two axes are

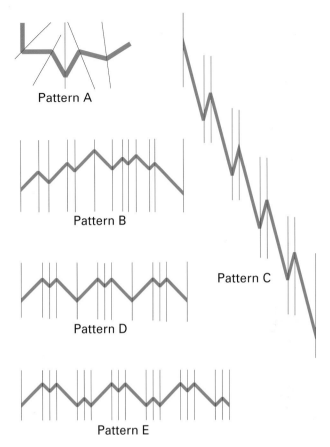

Figure 26. NONSTANDARD DESIGNS FROM A LINEAR LAMINATE

perpendicular to each other, but the pattern repeats itself every four sections rather than every two. The same general results are obtained if one wide section is alternated with two narrow sections or vice versa (see Pattern E, Figure 26). However, this design repeats itself every six sections. There are many other combinations of this type that are possible.

Another variation is to assemble cross sections cut from mitered laminates in which the cuts are made through the same type of, but not adjacent, center points. For example, cut every other A-point, making each cross section double the standard width. Or make the cuts at every third center point. Cross sections of the same width are assembled, or two or more different ones are combined in some regular fashion for a different design.

Figure 27. THE EFFECT ON THE DESIGN OF STANDARD VERSUS NONSTANDARD CROSS SECTIONS

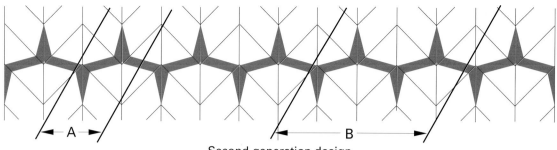

Second-generation design

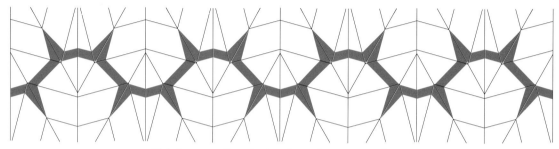

Third-generation design from A cross sections

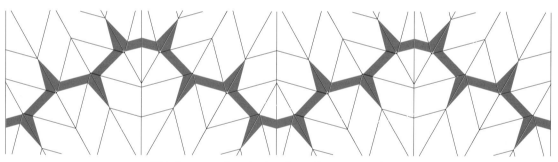

Third-generation design from B cross sections

Figure 27 (top) shows a mitered laminate made by the standard procedure. When these A-sections, consisting of single repeating design units, are converted to the next generation, the design in the center of the drawing is produced. Cutting each section two repeating design units wide results in the design shown at the bottom. With three repeating design units, the resulting design will be different from either of the other two.

UNMATCHED STRIPES

In the standard procedure, every other section is turned over before the sections are glued together. If none are turned over before gluing, the sections can be glued together in a variety of ways. However, it is not possible to match or connect the stripe in going from one section to the other. The result when cutting a linear laminate is a series of parallel diagonal stripes; this is an example of

Figure 28. NONSTANDARD AND NONCONTINUOUS DESIGNS

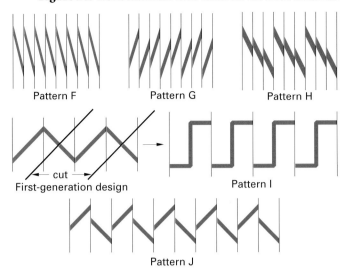

Pattern F

Pattern G

Pattern H

cut

First-generation design

Pattern I

Pattern J

the type of wood decoration carried out by woodworkers in the past. The stripes can all be lined up (Pattern F, Figure 28). They can be alternately placed in pairs at a high and a low level (Pattern G, Figure 28). They also can be alternated in groups of three, as in Pattern H, Figure 28. Either a standard or a nonstandard laminate can be used for making these nonstandard laminates. Many other variations of this type are possible; all produce discontinuous designs.

Following the same procedure with a first-generation laminate, a different design is created when the pattern is cut into cross sections, but none are turned over before assembly. Instead, sections are lined up, side by side, and glued together. A disconnected design is the result (Pattern I, Figure 28).

Another variation is to follow the standard procedure but without matching up the design, displacing the design in an orderly fashion. A variety of different, repeatable patterns can result, but the designs are not continuous. Pattern J in Figure 28 is an example of one such design. Again, either type of laminate may be used. The vase in Photo 1 (page 94) shows some of the above designs.

OFF-CENTER CUTS

First-generation and higher-generation mitered laminates have only two cutting points in each repeating pattern that will give a standard design. If the cuts are made at some other point, the resulting pattern may be similar to the standard design, but not symmetrical. To do this, cut a zigzag pattern at 60° at the locations shown at the top of Figure 29. One cut should be at the midpoint of either the ascending or descending leg; these are the standard points (A and D locations). The other cuts are halfway between the standard points and the lower apexes of the design (B and C locations).

Pattern K, the standard design, is produced when the cuts are made through the A-points. However, when the cuts are not made through corresponding center points but through the B-points (as shown in the drawing), two different designs will result. This is possible because cross sections can be assembled and glued together in two different configurations. This results in two patterns—LA and LB. These are no longer symmetrical with respect to the longitudinal axis. One (Pattern LB) is also not symmetrical with respect to the glue lines. Only when cuts are made through corresponding center points are the resulting designs fully symmetrical.

The next three patterns (Patterns M, NA, and NB in Figure 29) show the designs achieved when cuts are made through corresponding points on the descending legs of a design. The standard cuts (through the D-points) result in the standard design shown as Pattern M. Cross sections made by cutting through the nonstandard C-points can produce two designs (NA and NB). The same general comments apply to these designs as to those made about the ones resulting from cuts through the ascending legs of the design.

When the midpoints of the ascending and descending legs are both cut, Pattern O is the standard design. Cutting both legs only 25% of the way up (at the B-points and the C-points) produces Pattern P. Cutting the zigzag laminate at other points results in similar, though different, designs. These are just a few examples of the changes in pattern resulting from this change in the process.

Only a sampling of the many possibilities for making nonstandard designs—in which only one step in the procedure is nonstandard—are described in this chapter. If two or more of the standard steps in the procedure are not followed, many other nonstandard designs are created. All of these nonstandard designs, when they are symmetrical, can be converted into next-generation, nonstandard designs by either standard or nonstandard procedures. The resulting designs can be converted to new designs by repeating the procedure.

Figure 29. THE EFFECT ON THE DESIGN OF STANDARD VERSUS NONSTANDARD CUTS

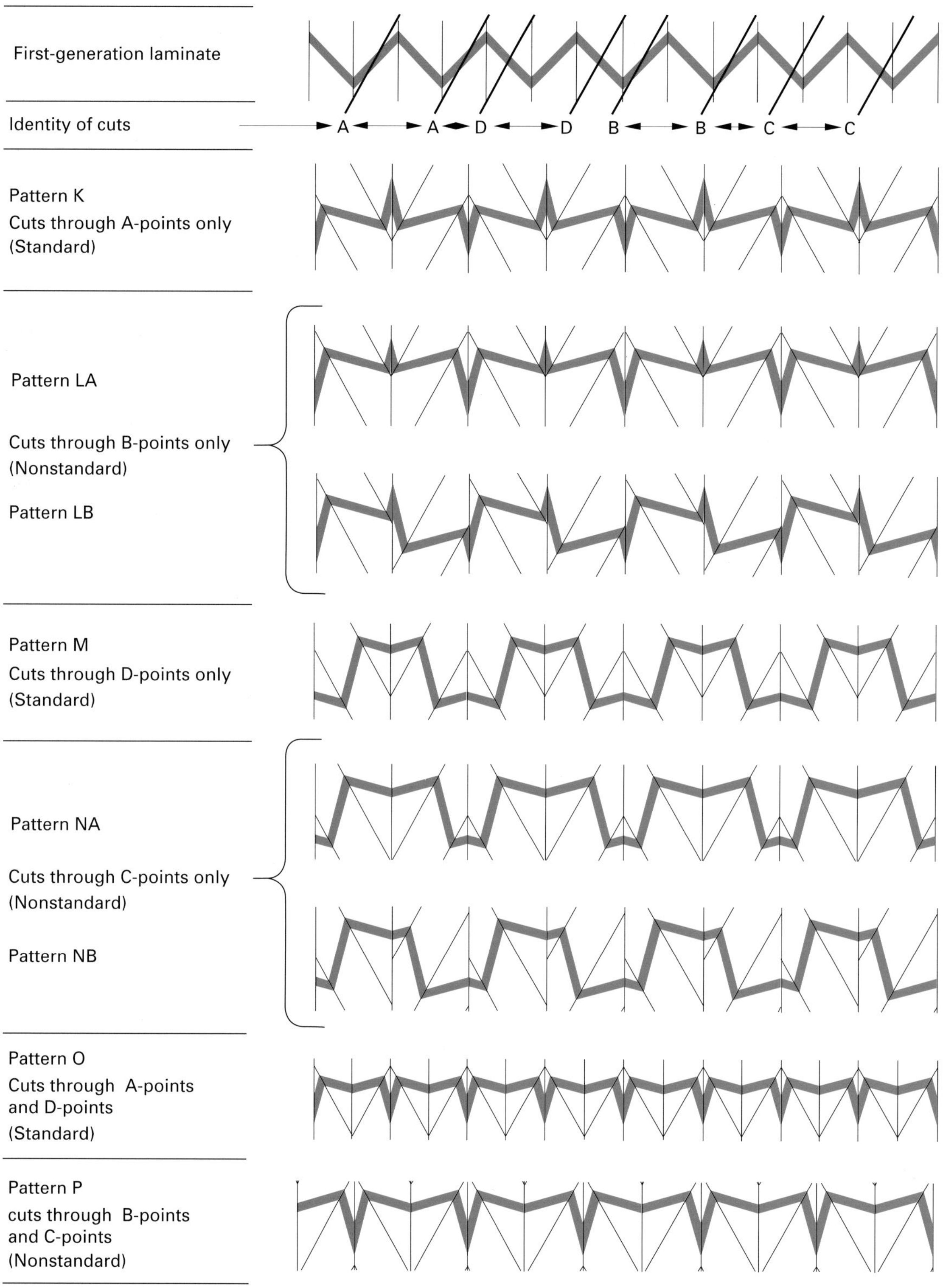

First-generation laminate

Identity of cuts

Pattern K
Cuts through A-points only
(Standard)

Pattern LA

Cuts through B-points only
(Nonstandard)

Pattern LB

Pattern M
Cuts through D-points only
(Standard)

Pattern NA

Cuts through C-points only
(Nonstandard)

Pattern NB

Pattern O
Cuts through A-points
and D-points
(Standard)

Pattern P
cuts through B-points
and C-points
(Nonstandard)

ADDED PROCESS STEPS

There are many ways to make other nonstandard designs, either from standard or nonstandard patterns. These involve making the mitered laminate, then using one or two extra steps to convert it to a design that is nonstandard. This book briefly describes a few of these.

The diamond design is one example. It is easily made from a steep zigzag pattern. Cut the zigzag laminate into two halves along its longitudinal center line. Shift one half of the cut laminate a distance equal to the width of a cross section and glue them back together. Figure 30 (Pattern Q) illustrates the process.

Another method is to cut off two zigzag laminates longitudinally along the tips of their upper or lower apexes (Pattern R, Figure 30). Glue these together along the cut edges to form diamond designs. These designs are connected. If the apexes are completely cut off, the resulting diamond designs are not connected. Both of the above two diamond designs can be seen in the cutting board, page 76 (right).

Square designs (separated by a space) are made in the same fashion as above with one exception. Here the starting laminate is the second-generation design 45/45D. Cut this design into two halves along its longitudinal axis. Offset the two halves by the width of a section and reglue. This results in square patterns separated by the width of a section, shown as Pattern S in Figure 30.

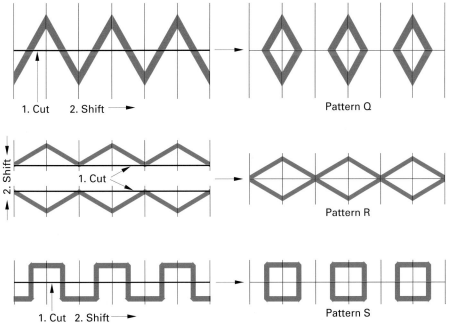

Figure 30. NONSTANDARD CLOSED DESIGNS MADE BY CUTTING A DESIGN, SHIFTING PART OF IT, AND REGLUING

1. Cut   2. Shift ——→   Pattern Q

2. Shift   1. Cut   Pattern R

1. Cut   2. Shift ——→   Pattern S

Instead of cutting the 45/45D pattern into halves, cut off only the upper horizontal part of one design and the lower part of the other. Reglue the two cut edges. The result is rectangular designs (Pattern T, Figure 31). Pattern U in Figure 31 (see Photo 1, page 94) requires a broad stripe. It must be wider than the width of the cross sections. Glue the crosscut sections side by side without turning any over. Cut the design into halves longitudinally (center figure). Turn one half end over end and glue the two cut edges together.

An arrow design is made by gluing the cross sections cut from a linear laminate side by side without turning any of the sections over. Cut the parallel stripe design into two halves along its longitudinal axis. Turn one half end over end and glue it to the other half. The design (Pattern V, Figure 31) is discontinuous. Chevrons can be made in the same manner when the process is begun by cutting the linear laminate at a smaller angle.

Figure 31. MORE NONSTANDARD DESIGNS MADE BY CUTTING A DESIGN, SHIFTING PART OF IT, AND REGLUING

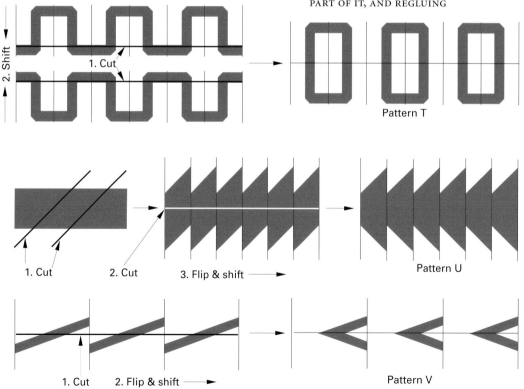

Chapter 11

Applications

As I have mentioned, there is great potential for using mitered laminate designs in fields other than woodworking. This chapter will discuss who can benefit from this process, and which industries can use the designs to expand and improve their products.

The main emphasis in the previous chapters was on the *process* of making mitered laminates. In woodworking, the process and the resulting designs are closely integrated and related; in other applications, the two are not as closely related, although both are important, and it is the designs and patterns that are the justification for the process itself. In this chapter, the primary emphasis will be on the application of these designs and patterns to various consumer products.

Outlined below is a list of suggestions for how to use mitered laminate designs. A more detailed discussion of each follows.

1. The design is developed in the product during or as part of the manufacturing process.
   a. By following the mitered laminate process using a particular material
   b. By combining design elements, row-by-row or course-by-course, as the product is made

2. The design is applied to or on the product.
   a. By printing the design on the product
   b. By cutting out parts or elements of the design from different-colored or different-textured materials and fitting the parts together into the design
      i. Unite the parts into the design piece-by-piece
      ii. Unite the parts at the job site, one-by-one, as they are being attached to a base
      iii. Unite the parts onto squares of disposable material and glue these to a base or embed them in mortar on a base
      iv. Unite the parts onto a square or sheet base and integrate these into a unit in a manufacturing process

Designs Developed During the Process

The first method that can be used to develop a design during the manufacturing process applies to woodworkers and is the basis for most of the material in prior chapters. The basic process starts with a board, with or without a stripe, laminated or nonlaminated. Following the mitered laminate procedure, the board is converted into a mitered laminated board with a design or pattern and is used to create or enhance a wooden item. In addition to the items already mentioned, woodworkers can enhance furniture, architectural woodwork, wood flooring, and related items.

Mitered laminate designs can be used to enhance wood flooring. The most logical application, it seems, is the use of mitered laminates as a border around a regular plank floor or as a central medallion in a floor. When used in this way, the size of the design is normally larger than designs made for other applications. Thus, this application requires more sophisticated machinery than is needed for small-scale mitered laminate designs; this machinery is sometimes computerized and always requires training and expertise to operate.

Incorporating a mitered laminate design into a wood floor would require the same technique as making a design for a cutting board or tray. Though such a floor has, to my knowledge, never been made, the final result can be depicted with a drawing. Figure 1 shows a plan of a 60/30AD design being used as a border and a round central medallion. The large scale makes it difficult to see the actual design in the drawing; Figure 2 shows a detail of a corner of the border design.

Figure 1. A FLOOR DECORATED WITH A BORDER AND A CENTER MEDALLION MADE FROM A 60/30AD DESIGN

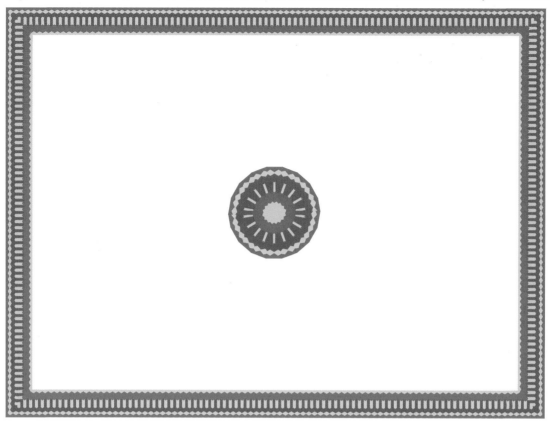

DEVELOPING THE DESIGN IN TEXTILES

The other method for developing a design while making a product applies to textile consumer goods. The design is woven in, a row or a course at a time. The most common example is the manufacture of carpets and designer rugs. Other examples include textile fabrics made on a Jacquard loom or similar machine. Mitered laminate designs would provide the textile industry with a variety of new and unique designs.

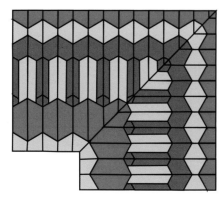

Figure 2. AN ENLARGED VIEW OF A CORNER OF THE FLOOR DESIGN

Application of Designs on a Product

Products can be decorated with mitered laminate designs without the product going through the mitered laminate process. In this case, the design is created from a material, then applied to the item. There are two general methods for accomplishing this. In one, the design is simply printed or transferred onto the item. In the other, the elements of the design are cut out of different-colored or different-textured material, fitted together in some manner, then used as is or attached to a solid base.

THE PRINTING METHOD

Printing has the most potential for utilizing mitered laminate designs for decorative purposes. Many printing techniques can be used to transfer the design to the product. Almost any consumer item that is decorated or enhanced before being sold is suitable for application of mitered laminate designs; this process expands the number of designs that a manufacturer can produce and sell.

The items that can be decorated include sheets or panels used in the construction industry (countertops, printed laminates, and ceiling panels), textiles of all varieties (wearables, piece goods, rugs, draperies, bedding and linens, and upholstery), plastic products (panels, sheets, film, home decorating items, home accessories, upholstery, and draperies), tableware (china, napkins, and place mats), and paper products (wallpaper, shelf liners, disposable household products, and home decorating items).

The use of quilt patterns as designs on wallpaper is becoming increasingly popular. Although there are about 4,000 documented wall quilt patterns, the use of designs made by the mitered laminate process would provide additional types or styles of patterns for wallpaper manufacturers.

THE CUTTING-OUT AND FITTING-TOGETHER METHOD

In this method, elements or sections of the design are cut out of different-colored or different-textured material. These pieces are then fitted together and bonded or united into a continuous design or pattern.

Although fabrics with quilt designs can be printed with mitered laminate designs, an alternative is to use the cutting-out and fitting-together method. Instead of gluing sections together (as with wood), the pattern pieces or parts are joined by stitching. The process can be used by amateur quilters, quilting professionals, and quilt manufacturers alike. The mitered laminate process provides them with a large variety of additional patterns.

Though no one has made a quilt using the designs in this book, I have tried to portray what a quilt would look like made with 100 blocks of 30/60A designs and fitted with a border (Figure 3). The design of a quilt block is shown in Figure 4—each patch that makes up the block is numbered. The outlines of the various shapes are illustrated in Figure 5 (page 112), and the number required to make a block is indicated.

Another simple method of attaching the pieces or elements of the design to a base is to glue them, one piece at a time, to the application area. Although simple, this procedure is labor intensive, time consuming, and costly. Nevertheless, it is currently being used for covering floors, walls, and countertops, and when using standard materials to make borders in expensive homes and businesses. This technique is gaining popularity, because patchwork quilt patterns are being used. They have become *designer patterns*, because the designs are new and different from the ones normally sold for these applications. Mitered laminate designs are different from either and can be applied using the same technique. However, there are less costly ways of achieving the same results.

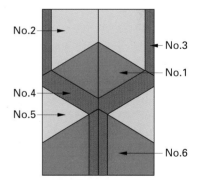

Figure 4. A QUILT BLOCK MADE WITH A 30/60A DESIGN; THE DIFFERENT TYPES OF PATCHES ARE INDICATED

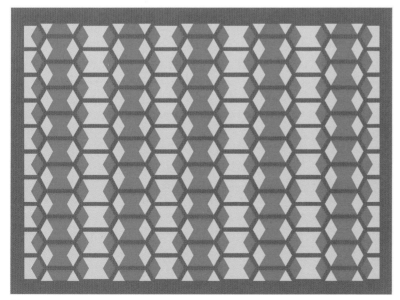

Figure 3. WHAT A QUILT WOULD LOOK LIKE IF MADE FROM 100 BLOCKS OF A 30/60A DESIGN AND FITTED WITH A BORDER

Figure 5. SHAPE AND NUMBER OF THE DIFFERENT PATCHES
REQUIRED FOR ONE QUILT BLOCK

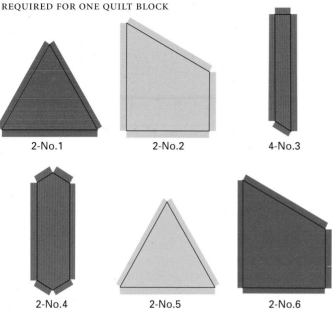

2-No.1	2-No.2	4-No.3
2-No.4	2-No.5	2-No.6

Who Can Use Mitered Laminate Designs?

A method that is much less labor intensive is the technique used to install ceramic tile. The pieces making up the design are attached to disposable backing squares, which hold the pieces in place. With ceramic tile, the squares are set in mortar. Other materials, such as vinyl sheets, plastic laminates, and carpeting could be cut into pieces for a pattern, fitted together, and glued to a backing such as burlap and then onto a floor, wall, or countertop. These squares fit together on a base so that the design extends in all directions. After the mortar or glue has set, the backing squares are stripped off.

Even less costly is *inlaying* the mitered laminate pieces or elements of the design. In this case, inlaying does not mean fitting a strip of wood into a groove or dado cut into a flat wood surface. It gets its name from "inlaid linoleum" in which the design and color go all the way through. In this technique, different-colored design pieces are fitted together into a connected pattern on top of a base material or substrate. The substrate can either be small squares or long sheets. The substrate and the design pieces are integrated into flat tiles or sheets in a manufacturing process and glued to the surface to be covered.

Note that the cutting-out and fitting-together method normally produce surfaces that are more wear- and scuff-resistant than designs applied by the printing method.

There are, in general, four categories of people who can benefit from mitered laminate designs: tradespeople, hobbyists, people in technical fields, and pattern designers. The first two usually are self-employed and work alone or in a small group. Generally, they are not only familiar with all aspects of the laminate process but know how to combine the designs with the products. They participate in all of the work connected with enhancing a product with mitered laminate designs. This would apply to most woodworkers, quilters, crafters, artists, floor-covering installers, and other small-shop owners.

People in technical fields and pattern designers are normally salaried employees who work for large companies. Artists, designers, engineers, planners, and others with technical degrees are often qualified and interested in this type of work. Regardless of the size of the business, those responsible for the designs must understand the principles involved in creating designs using the mitered laminate process. Making designs with paper or on a computer is very helpful in creating and changing designs (see chapter 8). Being able to make designs to a specific size (see chapter 9) is useful in all applications and a necessity in some.

In general, anyone who is interested in design can understand all aspects of the mitered laminate process, with the possible exception of sizing. An understanding of mathematics is needed for this aspect of the craft (see chapter 9). If an individual is responsible for conceiving and choosing designs for application, he or she will need more than a knowledge of the mechanics or technical aspects of the process. The individual should have an inherent or intuitive appreciation of the type of designs pleasing to the customers.

Artists, hobbyists, and others can make designs for their own pleasure or entertainment. These individuals could apply mitered laminate designs to creations of their own, which are made for either display or sale. Experimenting with and creating new designs can be recreational and fulfilling as well as profitable.

Chapter 12
Projects

Now that you know the basic techniques for making mitered laminate designs, it's time you tried your hand at a project. This chapter will lead you through five projects. The first project is a cheese board and is the simplest and easiest to make, requiring relatively little time and equipment. The next project is a candle box and is somewhat more difficult and time consuming. The other projects are progressively more difficult, more time consuming, and require the application of additional technology. The last two, a tray and a game table, require considerable planning so that the designs fit the specific areas of the project. The table is an advanced project and is recommended only for more experienced woodworkers.

Cheese Board

In the first project, a simple, easy-to-make laminate is incorporated into a cheese board, which is cut into the shape of a fish. The mitered laminate to be made for this project is a nonstandard second-generation laminate with a 45/75 design. It is used in the same way as in making a narrow border around a planar object with straight sides. Only two laminated cross sections are used for a cheese board. The mitered laminate design is made first, then glued between two pieces of a suitable hardwood; then it is cut out into the shape of a fish.

The Design

The first step is making a linear laminate. The chosen design, 45/75, is made from this laminate in a two-step process. Glue two boards together, side by side; each piece should be 3 inches (7.5 cm) wide, ¾ inch (2 cm) thick, and 30 inches (76 cm) long. This is normally enough laminate to make several cheese boards. It also permits you to make a few mistakes in cutting sections or gluing them together. Use one walnut and one maple board. Photo 1 (left side) shows what the two boards look like after they have been glued together.

Photo 1 also shows how the next step is carried out. The linear laminate is cut at 45° into ½-inch (1.5-cm) cross sections. The photograph shows the laminate being cut into sections on the sliding table cutoff jig described in chapter 3. This is the method I use for making these cuts in order to get the accuracy and precision required for making glue joints that are nearly invisible. (The techniques I use are also described in this chapter.) It is not necessary to use a saw with this type of attachment if you have another procedure for making these cuts that meets your requirements. These cuts can also be made on a table saw with a miter jig or on a radial arm saw. Using a miter box is also an option.

The next step is arranging these cut sections properly before gluing them into a first-generation laminate. How the cutoff sections are arranged is shown in Photo 1 (lower center). On the left, the sections are arranged as they were in the linear laminate before being cut into sections. On the right, every other section has been turned end over end. Several sections have been pushed together and matched to illustrate what a properly arranged first-generation laminate looks like.

Arrange all the sections in this manner by alternately turning over sections. In positioning the sections for gluing, nowhere should the walnut in one section come in contact with walnut in any other section. The same holds true for the maple. The walnut and the maple should alternate, going from the right to the left and from the top to the bottom. Glue all the sections together, clamp, and allow to dry thoroughly (Photo 2). This produces a nonstandard first-generation laminate design. It is nonstandard for two reasons: the laminate does not have a stripe as defined in this book, and the two outboard planks are not the same. The glued laminate has sharp points along both edges. These points can be cut off so that the two edges are straight and smooth—they have not been cut off in this photo. The two sides are sanded flat and smooth. This laminate is used for making the second-generation laminate.

Photo 1. THE LINEAR LAMINATE FOR THE CHEESE BOARD BEING CUT INTO CROSS SECTIONS AT 45°

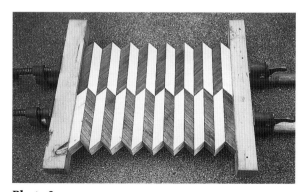

Photo 2. THE CROSS SECTIONS FROM A LINEAR LAMINATE GLUED TOGETHER TO FORM A NONSTANDARD FIRST-GENERATION LAMINATE

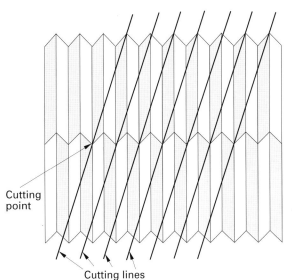

Figure 1. WHERE CUTS ARE MADE TO CREATE A LAMINATE FOR THE CHEESE BOARD

The next step is to convert this first-generation laminate into a second-generation design. The laminate is cut into cross sections at 75°. Nonstandard cuts are used for making this laminate. They are made through points where four mitered pieces come together. Figure 1 illustrates where these cuts are made. Making the cuts exactly and repeatedly through the center of this point is difficult without some way of accurately positioning the laminate. I use a procedure that requires the use of a *stretched-wire* or *scribed-line jig* attached to a sliding table cutoff jig. How these jigs are made and used is fully explained in chapter 3; please refer to this chapter for guidance unless you have another method that will provide the desired results. The positioning jig, the scribed-line model, and the cutting operation are depicted in Photo 3.

Photo 3 also shows how pairs of cross sections are positioned to produce the two-part laminate that will be incorporated into the cheese board. One of the sections is turned side over side and positioned against the other so that the walnut and the maple pieces in one section exactly match the same wood species in the other. Glue a pair of these sections together as in Photo 4. Once the glue has dried thoroughly, sand the sides flat. Glue

Photo 3. THE FIRST-GENERATION LAMINATE BEING CUT INTO SECTIONS AT 75° TO CREATE A SECOND-GENERATION DESIGN

this two-section laminate between two pieces of walnut as shown in Photo 5. The walnut boards should be of the same thickness as the laminate and at least large enough for the cheese board design. After the glue has dried, sand both sides of these glued-up boards before proceeding to the next step.

Although I chose a fish as the shape for this board, a cheese board can be made in the shape of a variety of objects. For the shape in the photograph, cut out a fish design from paper. Attach this design to the glued-up boards with pieces of tape as shown in Photo 6. With a band saw or scroll saw, cut out the fish design from the board. Photo 7 shows the board after it has been cut out. Sand the edges all around the fish. To complete the project, drill a ¾-inch (2-cm) hole for the fish's eye. Glue a ½-inch (1.5-cm) diameter piece of dowel as long as the thickness of the board into the fish's eye socket. Sand the entire fish and complete the project by putting on a finish.

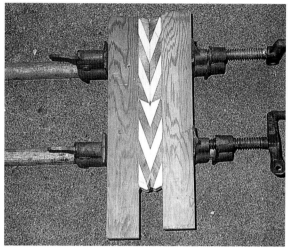

Photo 4. TWO OF THE SECOND-GENERATION CROSS SECTIONS GLUED TOGETHER FOR THE CHEESE BOARD DESIGN

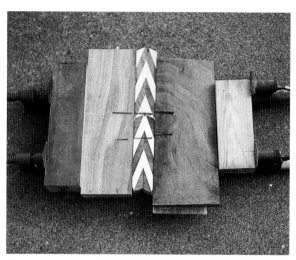

Photo 5. THE BONDED TWO-SECTION LAMINATE GLUED BETWEEN TWO PIECES OF WALNUT

Photo 6. THE OUTLINE OF A FISH (ON A PIECE OF TRANSPARENT PAPER) IS TAPED TO THE LAMINATE.

Photo 7. THE LAMINATED BOARD AFTER BEING CUT OUT WITH A BAND SAW

Candle Box

Project 2: CANDLE BOX
WITH MITERED LAMINATE
TOP; 13½ X 5¼ X 4¾ INCHES
(34 X 13 X 12 CM); CHERRY,
WALNUT, AND TWO
UNKNOWN WOOD SPECIES

This project is somewhat more demanding than the cheese board. The overall laminated design is larger, requiring many more sections of laminate and, thus, more time to make. Simply put, the process consists of first making a box, then making a top for it. A mitered laminate is used as the top. A convenient size for a candle box is 13 inches (33 cm) long, 4 inches (10 cm) wide, and 3 inches (7.5 cm) deep. The laminated top must thus be about 13 x 4 inches (33 x 10 cm). The sides of the box should be about ³⁄₁₆ inch (6 mm) thick. The top and bottom should be slightly thicker.

Making the Box

The box can be made from any appropriate hardwood, but it should blend with the woods used in making the top. This project was made mostly from cherry. The six parts that are used to make a candle box are shown in Photo 8. (Note that the top shown in this picture is not the one that is described below.) The sides of the box should be about ³⁄₁₆ inch (6 mm) thick. Two pieces, each 3 inches (7.5 cm) wide and 13 inches (33 cm) long, are cut for the sides, and two pieces having the same width but that are only 4 inches (10 cm) long are cut for the ends.

Photo 8. THE SIX PARTS USED
IN MAKING A CANDLE BOX

Cut small box or finger joints in each end of the four pieces of cherry. Photo 9 shows a radial arm saw being used to cut finger joints into one end of the side pieces for the box. Cut the slots ¼ inch (5 mm) deep so that, when assembled, the ends protrude about 1/16 inch (2 mm). Glue the four pieces together into a rectangular configuration, making certain that the sides are square. Sand off the protruding ends of the fingers. Also sand the top and bottom edges of the box so that each is planar.

The bottom or base of the box is made from the same wood and should be about 5/16 inch (8 mm) thick. Cut the piece about 5/8 inch (1.6 cm) longer and wider than the outside of the assembled sides. The exact size depends on the ogee bit used for routing the four edges. A vast variety of sizes and styles of these bits is available. They are used for making decorative edges on furniture, plaques, frames, and so forth. The bits cut a double curve, which is a combination of a concave and a convex line joined together.

After routing, the flat top of the base should be about ⅛ inch (3 mm) longer and ⅛ inch (3 mm) wider than the outside dimensions of the box. The flat part of the bottom will thus protrude 1/16 inch (2 mm) beyond the outside of the box. Center the base and glue it to the sides of the box, using clamps to make sure the box dries correctly. Photo 10 shows the base being glued to the sides.

Making the Top

The top of the box is made from a mitered laminate design. A nonstandard and unsymmetrical design was chosen for this mitered laminate. It is nonstandard because the two outboard planks used in making the linear laminate are different. Choose woods in contrasting colors for the outboard planks. The wood types should, however, work visually with the cherry used in the box itself and with the wood used for the stripe.

A 45/25A laminate was chosen for the box's top. The top should be made about ¾ inch (2 cm) thick. The first step in the process is to make a linear laminate about 36 inches (91.5 cm) long. This is normally more than required for this box, but it allows you to make several bad cuts. The laminate is made up of a stripe and two outboard planks. Make the stripe from a piece of walnut that is ⅛ inch (3 mm) x ¾ inch (2 cm) x 36 inches (91.5 cm) long. Each outboard plank should be ¾ inch (2 cm) thick by 1½ inches (4 cm) wide and 36 inches (91.5 cm) long.

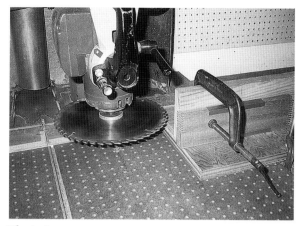

Photo 9. CUTTING FINGER JOINTS IN THE ENDS OF THE FOUR SIDES OF THE CANDLE BOX WITH A RADIAL ARM SAW

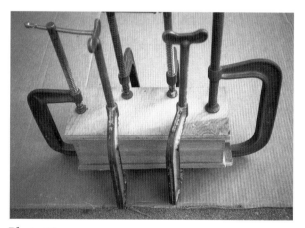

Photo 10. GLUING THE BOTTOM OF THE CANDLE BOX TO THE FOUR SIDES

Glue the walnut strip between the two outboard planks. The resulting linear laminate is thus 3⅛ inches (7.8 cm) wide, ¾ inch (2 cm) thick, and 36 inches (91.5 cm) long. This laminate can be seen in Photo 11 (left). To make a first-generation laminate, cut the linear laminate at 45° into ¾-inch-wide (2-cm) cross sections. I use a sliding table cutoff jig (described in chapter 3) to achieve the precision and accuracy needed for making nearly invisible joints. Other means can be used as long as the method produces satisfactory results. This cutting operation is shown in Photo 11. (*Note*: the laminate in the photo can be confusing, since the lightercolored wood reflects light differently, depending on the angle at which it is viewed; therefore, from one direction, it looks much lighter in color than from another direction.)

Photo 11. THE LINEAR LAMINATE FOR THE CANDLE BOX BEING CUT INTO CROSS SECTIONS TO MAKE A FIRST-GENERATION DESIGN

Photo 12. THE FIRST-GENERATION LAMINATE BEING CUT INTO CROSS SECTIONS FROM WHICH THE SECOND-GENERATION LAMINATE IS MADE

The cutoff cross sections must then be reassembled and oriented properly for gluing. Alternate cross sections are turned over before they are reassembled and glued. In this case, each alternate section is turned end over end as well as side over side. The properly oriented sections are shown in the lower right corner of Photo 11. Glue the sections together. In gluing the sections together, carefully match the walnut strip in each section with the stripe in each of the two adjoining sections.

Sand both sides of this laminate until flat and smooth. This is a first-generation mitered laminate and is used for making the next-generation design. In this assembly, the stripe forms a zigzag pattern with the darker and lighter woods in the outboard planks. This is shown in the glued-up laminate in Photo 12 (left).

The procedure for making the second-generation laminate is essentially the same as described above but with two exceptions. A different procedure must be used for cutting cross sections and for orienting the alternate cross sections for gluing. As before, the laminate that has just been made is cut into sections at an angle. Cut the laminate at 25° through its A-points into crosscut sections. To make the design, it must be cut through the exact center of each of the zigzag walnut stripes in which the stripe ascends or slopes upward.

The "A" in the code designates that the ascending or upward-slanting part of the stripe has been cut. Whether the cut has been made accurately can be easily tested. Turn the cutoff section side over side. Place it against the cutoff end of the laminate, matching the stripe in the two pieces. The pattern formed should be perfectly symmetrical with respect to the cut line. In other words, the design on one side of the glue line should be an exact mirror image of the pattern on the other side.

To judge by eye where to make this cut is very nonproductive. An error as small as 1/32 inch (1 mm) produces an imbalanced design. To solve this problem, I use a jig that is attached to the sliding table cutoff jig. One kind is a stretched-wire jig; the other one uses scribed lines for positioning the laminate on the sliding table. Both of them give satisfactory results, but the latter is much easier to adjust and is the one shown in the photo in Photo 12. Refer to chapter 3 for a detailed discussion of how to use either jig for cutting cross sections from second- and higher-generation laminates. Photo 12 shows the cutting operation.

After the first-generation laminate has been cut into cross sections, it is necessary to turn over every alternate cross section before the sections are glued together. Here, these sections need to be turned over only once—rather than in both directions. The alternates are turned side over side only. This process is illustrated in the lower right corner of Photo 12. On the left, the cutoff sections are first positioned as they were in the original laminate. On the right, alternate sections have been turned over and positioned into the desired configuration.

All the sections are then glued together in this manner. In the gluing process, the sections must be carefully matched with respect to the walnut stripe. The glued-up laminate, a 45/25A design, does not need to be longer than 7 inches (18 cm) for this project. Both sides are sanded until flat and smooth. The box top is made from this laminate.

The linear laminate has very uneven edges. Trim both edges of this laminate so that they are even and straight. Since this laminate was made much thicker than needed for the top, cut it into two halves on the band saw. Then glue the two halves together end to end, making a laminate twice its original length. Sand both sides of the glued-together laminate until they are planar and smooth.

Three styles of tops can be made from this second-generation laminate if it is as wide and long as the box itself. If it is that large, it can be cut to size and fitted. If it is not large enough to fit the box, then the top can be increased in width, or in length and width, to make it fit. In either case, strips of a matching wood, such as cherry, can be glued to both sides (or to all four) as required.

These strips of wood should be the same thickness as the top and at least ½ inch (1.5 cm) wide. When gluing strips to all four sides, the corners of the strips should be mitered. The box described above and pictured in the photo on page 117 has a ½-inch-wide (1.5-cm) cherry strip glued to all four edges.

Whatever style you are making, the next step is to sand both sides of the top to a thickness of ¼ inch (5 mm) or slightly less. Trim the top to fit the box, making it about ¹⁄₁₆ inch (2 mm) wider and longer that the outside dimensions of the box. Then cut a rabbet with a router ¹⁄₁₆ inch (2 mm) deep around the periphery of the bottom of the box's top. The rabbet should be just wide enough so that it just fits snugly inside the box. This completes the project except for sanding and applying a finish. Photo 13 shows other candle boxes with various mitered laminate designs.

Photo 13. ASSORTED CANDLE BOXES MADE USING THE SAME METHOD: LEFT, A THIRD-GENERATION DESIGN, 13¼ X 5½ X 4¼ INCHES (33.5 X 14 X 10.5 CM), FOUR UNKNOWN WOOD SPECIES; RIGHT, A SECOND-GENERATION DESIGN, 13½ X 5 X 5 INCHES (34 X 12.5 X 12.5 CM), WALNUT AND MAPLE

Clock

This project involves making a third-generation mitered laminate as well as converting this linear design into a circular configuration. This is done by cutting the laminate into a specific number of sectors or wedges, which are then glued together to make the circular design. The amount of laminate required for a clock is not large but the conversion from a second-generation to a third-generation laminate takes additional material. I started with enough linear laminate to make several clocks. Though the final designs were different for the various clocks, all were made from the same linear laminate. Here, I will describe how to make only a 60/45A/45A linear design and convert it into a circular pattern for the face of the clock.

The detailed procedures for making standard mitered laminates have been fully described in chapters 2, 3, and 4, as well as covered for some of the steps in the two projects already presented in this chapter. For this project and the ones to follow, the details of how to carry out the standard steps in the process will not be as detailed. However, the variables used for making a particular design will be given and discussed, if appropriate. Several procedures and considerations that must be observed, but that may not have been presented earlier, will be discussed fully.

As usual, the first step is to make a linear laminate from which all succeeding laminates will be made. Since I needed a number of feet of linear laminate to make several clock faces, I started with a linear laminate three times the thickness required for the project. This I cut into three thinner laminates, all having the same design and thickness.

I began with two pieces of walnut, each 3½ inches (9 cm) wide, 1½ inches (4 cm) thick, and 48 inches (122 cm) long for the outboard planks. I cut three boards 3½ inches (9 cm) wide, ⅛ inch (3 mm) thick, and 48 inches (122 cm) long for the stripe. I made two from maple and one from cherry. Any combination of woods can be used, but there should be considerable contrast in color between the woods and they should blend. Glue the five pieces of wood together, putting the cherry in the center, flanked on either side by a maple board. These stripes are then placed between the two pieces of walnut. This arrangement and the clamping operation are shown in Photo 14.

Project 3: CLOCK WITH MITERED LAMINATE DESIGN; 10 INCH (25.5 CM) IN DIAMETER AND ½ INCH (1.5 CM) THICK; WALNUT, MAPLE, AND CHERRY

Photo 14. THE BOARDS FOR A LINEAR LAMINATE FOR A CLOCK ARE GLUED TOGETHER AFTER GLUE IS APPLIED TO ALL MATCHING SURFACES.

If a large quantity of laminate is required for a project, there is a distinct advantage in making the linear laminate in the manner just described rather than making laminates of the desired thickness. Unless special care is exercised in making the linear laminate, the stripe in the laminate may not be truly perpendicular to the faces of the linear composite. If this is the case, the first and succeeding generations of laminates made from this linear laminate will not fit together properly. The stripe will not simultaneously match on both faces of the laminate. This is much more likely to happen when making a thin laminate—for example, one that is 1 inch (2.5 cm) thick—than when making one several times as thick. This problem can be avoided during the gluing process and can be corrected by proper planing.

The faces of the outboard planks that are perpendicular to the faces of the stripe must be glued together so that these faces lie in only two parallel planes, one on either side of the laminate. In other words, the outboard planks must not be offset one from the other. When these planks are offset and the laminate is planed to flatten its sides, the stripe will most likely no longer be perpendicular to the planed sides. After a laminate with offset outboard planks has been glued together, it is very difficult to correct the problem. The only way to correct it is to plane off both faces so that the faces of the outboard planks are perpendicular to the stripe. If the amount of misalignment is more at one end of the laminate than at the other, then it becomes nearly impossible to accurately square up the linear laminate.

I cut this laminate on the band saw into three narrower ones, each with the same thickness. The operation is depicted in Photo 15. These cuts can also be made with a table or radial arm saw or a circular saw. Each cut through a thick board would require two passes, one on each of the two sides. A sabre saw would also work if it has the capacity. Much more time and effort would be required by using any of these alternative methods. The cuts can even be made using a handsaw, though it would be tedious and time consuming.

Next, plane the cut faces of the three laminates until they are planar and of equal thickness. If you are making only one clock face, you will need only one of these narrower laminates. I used one of these linear laminates to make the clock face that is described below. Start by making the outboard planks 1½ inches (4 cm) wide,

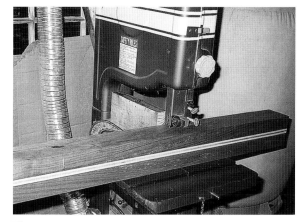

Photo 15. CUTTING A WIDE LINEAR LAMINATE INTO THREE NARROWER ONES ON THE BAND SAW

¾ inch (2 cm) thick, and 48 inches (122 cm) long. Make the three boards for the stripe ¾ inch (2 cm) wide, ⅛ inch (3 mm) thick, and 48 inches (122 cm) long.

As depicted in Photo 16, cut the linear laminate into cross sections ⅝ inch (1.6 cm) wide at a 60° angle. To arrange the cross sections correctly for the first-generation laminate, turn alternate sections over once. They can be turned either end over end or edge over edge. This process is demonstrated in the lower right corner of Photo 16. Proceeding towards the right, alternate sections are turned over and positioned side by side, matching the stripe at every adjoining section edge. This produces a zigzag pattern. Glue all the sections together in this manner, clamp, and allow to dry. Photo 17 shows the glued and clamped sections.

Photo 16. CUTTING THE LINEAR LAMINATE INTO CROSS SECTIONS FOR A FIRST-GENERATION DESIGN

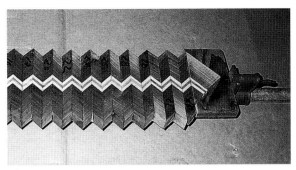

Photo 17. GLUING THE CROSS SECTIONS CUT FROM THE LINEAR LAMINATE INTO A FIRST-GENERATION DESIGN

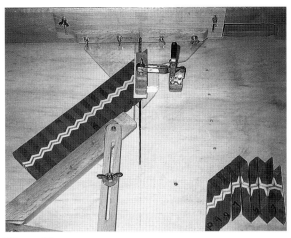

Photo 18. CUTTING THE FIRST-GENERATION LAMINATE INTO CROSS SECTIONS TO PRODUCE SECTIONS FOR MAKING A SECOND-GENERATION LAMINATE

As always, care must be taken in matching the stripes during glue-up. After the glue has dried, cut off the sharp points along both edges of the laminate so that the point where the edges meet is straight. Sand both sides of the laminate.

This first-generation laminate is then ready to be converted into a second-generation design. Cut the laminate into crosscut sections at 45° through the A-points. I used the scribed-line jig on the sliding table cutoff jig to cut off these sections (see chapter 3). Photo 18 shows how the sections are cut and how they are arranged prior to being glued into a second-generation laminate. This design is obtained by turning alternate cross sections either end over end or edge over edge. Use the standard method for gluing the section so as to produce the next-generation laminate. A standard method for gluing is simply to 1) turn over alternate cross sections, 2) position these side by side, and 3) glue them together, matching the stripe in each section with the stripes in the two adjoining sections. The clamping and arrangement can be seen in Photo 19.

After the glue has dried, trim off the sharp corners on the edges of the laminate. Sand both faces until each is flat and smooth. This produces a standard second-generation 60/45A mitered laminate and provides the starting material for making the next-generation design.

The procedure for this conversion is almost the same as for the one just described. These cuts are also made at 45° through the A-points. Photo 20 shows the cutting operation and how alternate cross sections are turned to achieve the desired design. There is one exception to the procedure for making the third-generation design. Alternate cross sections must be turned over twice—end over end, then edge over edge. The remainder of the

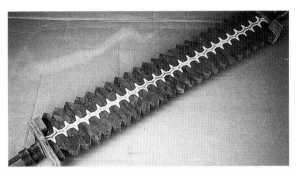

Photo 19. THE FIRST-GENERATION CROSS SECTIONS BEING GLUED INTO A SECOND-GENERATION LAMINATE

Photo 20. CUTTING THE SECOND-GENERATION LAMINATE INTO THIRD-GENERATION CROSS SECTIONS

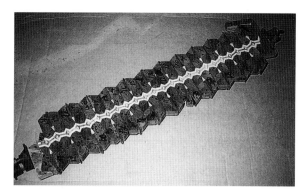

Photo 21. GLUING THE SECTIONS CUT FROM THE SECOND-GENERATION LAMINATE INTO A THIRD-GENERATION DESIGN

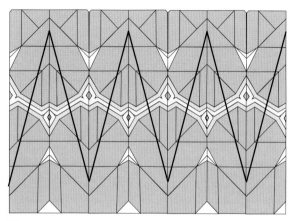

Figure 2. WHERE CUTS ARE MADE (HEAVIER LINES) TO CREATE WEDGES FOR THE CLOCK

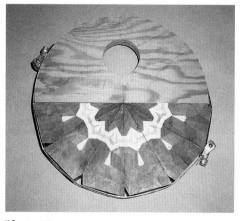

Photo 22. GLUING SIX LAMINATED WEDGES INTO A SEMICIRCULAR CONFIGURATION

operation is the same as above. The arrangement and clamping of the glued-up sections are depicted in Photo 21. This mitered laminate, a 60/45A/45A design, is then squared up and sanded as described above. This is the design used for the clock.

The mitered laminate is then converted from a linear design to a circular design. This becomes the clock's dial or face. This step will be detailed, since it has not been described in a previous project. In the first step, the linear mitered laminate is cut into pie-shaped pieces or wedges that, when fitted together, will make a circular pattern. A clock should be made with twelve wedges, one for each hour of the day. For these to fit accurately into a circle, each must be cut so that it has a 30° angle at its apex. This cutting angle or slope is calculated as follows:

$$\text{Cutting slope, degrees} = \frac{360°}{12 \text{ wedges}} \times \frac{1}{2} = 15°$$

Cutting it at 15° to the right and to the left gives a 30° angle. All cuts made in producing these wedges must go through successive central points of the stripe in each section of the linear mitered laminate.

Where these cuts are made is shown in Figure 2. Note that the cuts go through every center point, not alternate ones. These cuts can be easily and accurately made by using the sliding table cutoff jig fitted with a positioning jig. To cut these wedges, set and adjust the angle fence at 15°. Adjust the positioning jig (See chapter 3 for details) so that the cuts will go through the exact center of a leg of the design as depicted in Figure 2. Place the laminate firmly against the angle fence. Accurately position the laminate so that the cut will go through the center point of the design as described above. Clamp it in position and cut off the end piece. Unclamp the laminate and turn it over or upside down. Repeat this process, cutting through the next point. This produces the first wedge. Repeat the operation until six wedges have been cut.

In this process, only six wedges are needed for the clock. Arrange these into a semicircle as in Photo 22. To glue them together in this fashion, cut a piece of ¾ inch plywood into half of a circular disk with the same diameter as the wedges. Place the flat edge of the assembled wedges against the flat edge of the half-disk. Apply glue to the cut edges of the wedges, arrange, and clamp them to the half-disc with a circular clamp. The stripe in each wedge must match the one in the two adjoining wedges.

After the glue has dried, sand both sides of the semicircular laminate. Sand the straight edge so that it is planar and perpendicular to the faces of the laminate.

On a band saw, cut the semicircular laminate into two halves of equal thickness (Photo 23). Glue these two halves together along their flat edges, matching the stripe in one half with the stripe in the other half. Sand both faces of this circular laminate until each face is planar and smooth. Then cut it into a circle and sand the edges. Apply a finish. This is the face or dial of the clock.

Drill a hole in the center of the face. The hole should fit the stem of the clock movement to be installed. Attach the clock movement to the back of the clock's face. (Clock movements come with a complete set of instructions for installation.) Fit the hands to the clock and insert the battery. Set the time on the clock, and it is ready to be used or given as a gift.

Photo 23. THE SEMICIRCULAR LAMINATE IS CUT INTO TWO HALVES ON THE BAND SAW

Tray

Before you begin any project, you will need to decide the size of the piece and how it will be put together. This project is a rectangular tray with a low perpendicular rim around its outer edges and a built-in handle at each end. The bottom of the tray is decorated with a mitered laminate design. The dimensions for this tray are 12 inches wide by 15½ inches long with a 1-inch-high rim. *Note*: For this project, I think metric conversions are more confusing than helpful, so I have left them out. You can, however, convert from my units of measurement to metric units and the calculations will be exactly the same.

The first step is to select a design that is suitable for decorating a tray. The design can be selected from the examples given in chapter 4 (pages 33 through 61), or you can create it yourself, using one of the mitered laminate methods described in chapter 8. A 45/60A laminate, a second-generation design, was chosen for this project. The composition of the stripe is another facet of the design that must be selected. A five-strip stripe was chosen for this tray. There are two styles suitable for a tray. One is a linear design that extends from one end of the tray to the other. The other is a border design, extending along each of the four sides of the tray. The latter was chosen here.

The selection of a border design presents a problem that was not a concern in the previous projects. The laminate design has to be sized so that it fits the tray's dimensions. If this is not done, the tray could turn out to be either smaller or larger than desired. If, however, you have had considerable experience making a variety of designs, it is not that difficult to guess how wide to cut the cross sections from a linear laminate so that the design will be the proper size. This requires the use of some of the formulas that I have developed and described in chapter 9. The critical design factors needed to make a design that fits the tray—what formulas are used and how they are applied—will be discussed in detail.

Before construction of this project can begin, there are three design criteria that must be obtained. One is the composition of the stripe in the design. Another is how long the linear laminate must be to provide adequate material to complete the project. Third, determine what width the linear laminate cross sections must be cut to in order to make a design to the correct size. The first of these values is chosen; the other two have to be calculated.

Determining the Design Parameters

To make the design to a specific size, the width and height of a repeating design unit (RDU) must be determined. The height is chosen based on a scaled drawing of the tray and design. The width is determined from modeling the design. To model the design, with either paper or a computer, the specific design to be made and the total width of the stripe must be specified. Here, a 45/60A design with a ⅞-inch-wide stripe was selected. The width of the stripe affects the width of the design.

You may wonder how I come up with these variables. First, I try to picture in my mind what the tray, for example, should look like. What will be its physical characteristics? Will it be square, rectangular, or round? What size should it be? What type of rim would work best? Should it have handles, and, if so, where will they be located? What the tray will be used for may answer some of these questions.

If the tray is to be decorated with a mitered laminate design, there are a number of alternatives to be considered. Would it be more interesting to incorporate a linear, peripheral, or circular design into the tray's bottom? Look through the designs in chapter 4 for suitable ones. One design may be too wide, too dense, or too compact, while another may be too skimpy or too spread out.

Once you determine the type of design, next determine the composition of the stripe. The stripe should complement the design and provide balance. Should the stripe be bold or delicate? A bold design would call for a wide stripe with several strips. A delicate stripe should be narrower. You can adjust the strip—make it thicker or thinner—to achieve a different design. Once the stripe is decided on, choose the wood species and the width each strip will have. The wood strips should have a pleasing contrast, with respect to both color and size.

Draw the tray to scale, including the overall area to be occupied by the design as shown in Figure 3; the gray-shaded area represents this area. Measure the width of this area from the drawing. Based on the measurement in Figure 3, the design should be 3⁷⁄₁₆ inches wide. Make a model of the design, using either paper or the computer method. Figure 4 illustrates an individual, computer-generated RDU. (Note that Figure 4 actually shows the stripes in the design. This detail is not required for the purpose of determining the width to height ratio of the design.)

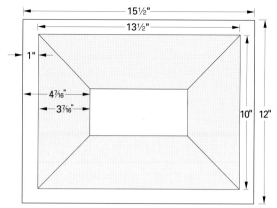

Figure 3. THE LOCATION (GRAY AREA) OF THE DESIGN IN THE TRAY

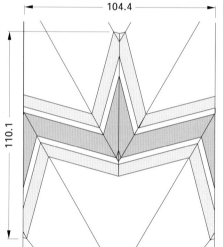

Figure 4. REPEATING DESIGN UNIT (RDU) FOR THE TRAY LAMINATE

Scale the width (104.4) to height (110.1) of the RDU (see above). The calculated ratio is 0.95. Note that this ratio is not affected by either the size of the design or the scale used in drawing it. From this ratio, calculate the width of an RDU by multiplying this ratio by the width of the design (3⁷⁄₁₆ inches). Thus, an RDU should be 3¼ inches wide.

Just to clarify: When the RDUs are connected side by side in a linear configuration, the individual RDU has the same width as the entire laminate. But when the RDU is considered an individual unit, the same dimension is called its *height*. The other dimension of this unit is designated as its *width*. This may be difficult to understand, but this nomenclature is based on the convention that the short side of a rectangle is called its width and the long side is either its height or length, depending on how the rectangle is viewed.

Project 4: TRAY WITH
MITERED LAMINATE DESIGN;
15½ X 12 X 1¾ INCHES
(39.5 X 30.5 X 4.5 CM);
POPLAR, CHERRY, WALNUT,
AND MAPLE

The following analogy should help explain the above anomaly. If you are looking at the picture of a person standing, the distance from left to right is called its width and the distance from the bottom to top its height. This would be like the drawing of an RDU in which most RDUs are taller than they are wide. Connect a number of these pictures together on the long sides, which is like gluing RDUs together to make a liner laminate. Now the short distance is its width and the long one is its length. Thus, the RDU dimension that was height is now width and what was originally called width is now length.

From the width of an RDU, the total number of RDUs required for the entire laminate can be determined. Divide the longest dimension of the design (13½ inches) by the width of the laminate (3¼ inches). This calculation gives 4.15 as the number of RDUs needed per side. Use the closest even whole number, or four, as the actual number of RDUs required. Use the same calculation for the shorter side of the tray. Divide 10 inches by 3¼ inches to obtain 3.08 as the number calculated. The next even whole number is four but that number of RDUs would make the design square rather than rectangular.

Normally, to make all the elements of a design fit at a mitered corner when configuring a polygon, the cuts must be made through the same center point and thus each side of the figure must have an even number of RDUs. There is a method that avoids these conditions. This method can be used here, since an odd number of RDUs are required for two of the sides. You will need to make transition or conversion pieces. This procedure is described in chapter 6 and illustrated in Figures 4 and 5 in that chapter. Thus, any number of RDUs can be used for either or both sides of a corner. Choose three as the number of RDUs for the short side.

The number of linear laminate cross sections needed for the design can now be calculated from the above data. Add the number of RDUs required for the four sides (4 + 3 + 4 + 3), which results in 14 as the total number of RDUs in the design. Since there are two 45/60A cross sections in each RDU, double 14, giving 28 as the number of 60/45A cross sections in the whole design. Double this number again to obtain 56 as the number of linear laminate cross sections for the entire design.

The above number multiplied by the length of linear laminate used for making one linear laminate cross section gives the total quantity of linear laminate in the design. This is determined by the use of two equations developed in chapter 9. (How to use these equations will be explained here.) The first step is to calculate the width of a cross section that has to be cut from the linear laminate to produce a second-generation cross section (45/60A design) that has the same height and half the width of an RDU as shown in Figure 4. For this calculation, use equation 8 from chapter 9 (page 89), since this is the equation applicable to a second-generation laminate. Note: though I use inches here, the equation works the same with metric measurements. The equation is:

$$^2W_L = \frac{(W_2 + W_K)}{2 \sin A_1}$$

where,

^2W_L = Width of cross sections to cut from linear laminate

W_2 = 1⅝ inches = Width of cross sections required for tray

W_K = ⅛ inch = Width of saw blade kerf

A_1 = 60° = Cutting angle of first-generation laminate

Therefore,

$$^2W_L = \frac{1⅝" + ⅛"}{2 \sin 60°}$$

$$= \frac{1¾"}{(2)(0.866)}$$

$$= \frac{1.75"}{1.732}$$

$$= 1.010"$$

The solution of the equation shows that the linear laminate needs to be cut into 1-inch-wide cross sections. To determine the length of linear laminate needed, use equation 4 from chapter 9 (page 88) along with the number of cross sections required. Equation 4 gives the length of linear laminate needed for each cross section.

$$L_L = \frac{(W_L + W_K)}{\sin A_L}$$

where,

L_L = Length of linear laminate needed per cross section

W_L = 1 inch = Width of cross section cut from linear laminate

W_K = ⅛ inch = Width of saw blade kerf

A_L = 45° = Cutting angle of linear laminate

Therefore,

$$L_L = \frac{1" + ⅛"}{\sin 45°}$$

$$= \frac{1⅛"}{(0.707)}$$

$$= \frac{1.125"}{0.707}$$

$$= 1.59"$$

Each cross section cut from the linear laminate requires 1.59 inches of laminate. To determine the total length of linear laminate needed, multiply the number of linear laminates in the total design (56) by the length of linear laminate in one cross section (1.59 inches). From the calculation, it is determined that 89 inches of linear laminate are required. There is some waste when the ends of the linear and the first-generation laminates are cut off. Add 10% for each conversion, or 20%, to the length of linear laminate that needs to be made. Adding 20% to 89 inches gives 107 inches as the total length of linear laminate needed for the project.

This, however, is not the actual amount of linear laminate that has to be made. The length required and the amount of work involved in making the mitered design can be cut essentially in half. The bottom of the tray needs to be only about ¼ inch thick. By starting with a laminate ¾ inch thick, the final design can be cut into two halves, thus doubling the amount of the final design available for the tray. Thus, the actual amount that has to be made is half of the calculated value of 107 inches, or 54 inches. Having determined this value, you can begin making the tray.

Making the Tray

The first step is to make a linear laminate about 4½ feet long and ¾ inch thick, with a stripe ⅞ inch wide. Use a walnut strip 5/16 inch thick and about 4½ feet long for the center of the stripe. For the strips next to the center, cut two pieces of maple, each 3/32 inch thick and as long as the strip of walnut. For the outside strips of the stripe, make two strips of cherry, each 3/16 inch thick. Cut all these ¾ inch wide. Make the outboard planks from poplar each 2 inches wide and ¾ inch thick. Glue the five strips and the two outboard planks together to form a linear laminate 4⅞ inches wide, ¾ inch thick, and about 4½ feet long. After gluing, plane both sides of the laminate.

The next step is to cut cross sections from the linear laminate. Use the sliding table cut-off jig described in chapter 3 and shown in Photo 24. Set the angle fence at 45° to the saw blade. Clamp the laminate against this fence and push the cutoff jig through the saw blade, cutting off the end. Set the stop fence for 1-inch-wide cross sections. After unclamping the laminate, position it firmly against both fences and cut off the first cross section. After each cut, the laminate is unclamped, pushed up against both fences, and reclamped. Photo 24 shows the cutoff jig and a few of the sections that have been cut off. Some of these cross sections have been turned upside-down and pushed together into the pattern of a first-generation laminate design. Repeat this until the entire linear laminate has been cut into 1-inch-wide sections.

In the next step, glue these sections together after turning every other section upside-down. Line up the stripe in each section with the stripe in the two adjoining sections. This forms the zigzag pattern shown in Photo 25, a first-generation laminate. Glue these sections together. Leave this assembly clamped until the glue has dried (see Photo 25). Then cut off the saw-toothed edges on the zigzag laminate and sand both sides. The two edges must be parallel to each other and perpendicular to the sides. The two sides must be planar and parallel. Normally, a joiner or planer can't be used on mitered laminates, because both split out short ends of the laminated wood. Sometimes you can get by on the joiner if the blades are very sharp and very shallow cuts are made. In general, laminates other than linear laminates should be only sanded, routed, sawed, and turned.

The first-generation laminate is then cut into sections for making the tray. At the same time, the transition

Photo 24. CUTTING THE LINEAR LAMINATE FOR A TRAY INTO CROSS SECTIONS FOR A FIRST-GENERATION DESIGN

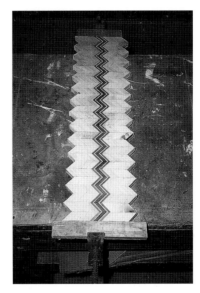

Photo 25. GLUING THE FIRST-GENERATION LAMINATE TOGETHER FROM CROSS SECTIONS CUT FROM THE LINEAR LAMINATE

pieces for making the corners of the design are cut. Where these cuts are made, as indicated by a dotted line, is shown in Figure 5; each section has been given a letter designation. Half of the tray requires four A-sections, two B-sections, and two C-sections. How these are fitted together is shown in Figure 6. In this figure, only a fourth of the total design is shown.

In making these cuts, use the sliding table cutoff jig with a centering attachment. Either version (chapter 3, Figure 3 or Figure 4) can be used. See Photo 26. Set the angle fence at 60° to the saw blade. Remove the stop fence as it is not needed for making these cuts. During this cutting operation, the two wires on the jig must always be maintained at an equal distance from the saw blade. The wires must also be parallel to each other, to the top

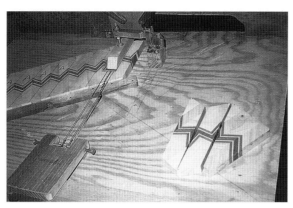

Photo 26. CUTTING THE FIRST-GENERATION LAMINATE INTO CROSS SECTIONS AND A CONVERSION PIECE FOR A SECOND-GENERATION DESIGN

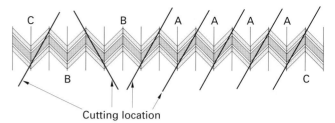

Figure 5. WHERE CUTS ARE MADE IN THE FIRST-GENERATION LAMINATE WHEN MAKING SECTIONS FOR THE TRAY DESIGN

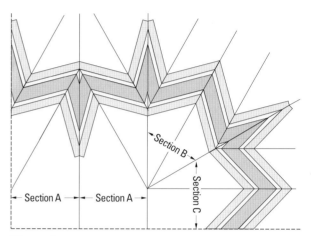

Figure 6. ONE-FOURTH OF THE ASSEMBLED DESIGN SECTIONS FOR THE TRAY

of the sliding jig, and to the saw blade. The distance of the wires from the top of the table must be the same as the thickness of the laminate.

Hold the laminate against the angle fence and position it under the wires so that the center of the ascending leg of the design is centered between the two wires. Adjust the wires so that each is directly over a corresponding point on the design, while maintaining all the conditions stated above. Corresponding points would be at either the outside or inside corners where the design changes direction. This usually requires considerable practice before the wires are properly positioned. Make a trial cut by placing the laminate against the fence. Position it properly underneath the wires then clamp it firmly in place. Cut the section off and check the cut by turning the cutoff piece upside-down and placing its cut edge against the cut edge of the laminate. Align the design on both sides of the joint. If one side of the joint is not a mirror image of the other side, the wires must be readjusted until a symmetrical design is produced.

After the wires have been properly adjusted, cut off sections. The cutting operation is shown in Photo 26. This cutting operation is not as routine as cutting standard laminate cross sections (such as cutting the four A-sections as shown in Figure 5, on the right). The first cut (on the far right of the drawing) produces a C-section. After cutting off four A-sections using the standard procedure, turn the laminate upside-down. Cut off the first B-section. Again, turn the laminate over and cut off the second B-section. Then cut the laminate at the glue line (at 90°) to make the second C-section. Four A-sec-

tions, two B-sections, and two C-sections are enough to make half of the full design. Assemble the sections as shown in Figure 6 by adding the same sections on the left in a mirror-image pattern. The arrangement is shown in Photos 27 and 28. This is half of the design for the tray bottom.

To simplify the gluing process, glue the sections together in stages. First, glue two corner sections (B-sections and C-sections) together as shown in Photo 27. Then repeat the process for the mirror-image part of the design. From each glued section, cut off the projecting end from the C-section seen in Photo 27 so that it is even with the cut edge of the B-section. Then glue the four standard cross sections (A-sections) between the two corner sections as shown in Photo 28. When gluing, keep the design accurately aligned at all glue joints.

As seen in Photo 28, the laminate does not extend completely to the corners. Glue on a strip of ¾-inch-thick poplar to each outside corner edge of the two B-sections to fill in the missing corners. Photo 28 also shows that there are three small triangular areas on the long edge that need to be repaired. If the outboard planks had been a little wider, these areas would have been filled in. Fit and glue a small triangular piece of wood in each area. Trim this patched laminate by cutting off the A-sections even with the cut edges of the C-sections. Using a large belt or edge sander, sand this edge until it is planar and perpendicular to the face of the laminate. Trim the opposite edge parallel to this sanded edge so that the laminate is 6 inches wide. Sand the two faces of the laminate.

Using a band saw, carefully saw this piece of laminate into two halves of equal thickness. Photo 29 shows the cutting operation. Sand the two cut faces and check the planarity of the joints to be glued. If the edges of the two halves do not match perfectly, carefully sand them until they do. Glue the two halves together, aligning the stripe on both sides of the joint. Photo 30 shows the tray bottom clamped together after gluing. After the glue has dried, sand the two surfaces of the tray bottom until smooth and planar. Square up the tray bottom, centering the design, by trimming it with a table or radial arm saw.

The rim of the tray was made from a laminate. Glue five 1-inch-wide strips about 31 inches long together in the following order: ½ inch poplar, ¼ inch cherry, ¹⁄₁₆ inch poplar, and ¼ inch walnut. With a band saw, cut this laminate into equal halves. Plane each half to a thickness of ⁵⁄₁₆ inch. Route a ⅛-inch by ¼-inch rabbet on one edge of each half. Cut each half into two pieces, one 13 inches long and the other 17 inches long. Cut a 45° miter on the end of each piece, making each the proper length to fit a side of the tray bottom.

Make a shallow cut along each 45° end-cut for inserting a spline. Fashion a handhold at the center of each end piece according to Figure 7. Rip off the top part of the long pieces so that they are the same width as the ends of the shorter pieces that have the handholds. Sand the four pieces. Glue these together with splines in the four corners, then glue this assembly to the tray bottom. After the glue has dried, sand the entire assembly. Then apply a clear finish, followed by a coat of wax.

Figure 7. DESIGN OF THE TRAY HANDLE

Photo 27. ONE CORNER OF THE TRAY DESIGN GLUED TOGETHER FROM TWO CUT FIRST-GENERATION CONVERSION PIECES

Photo 28. HALF OF THE COMPLETE DESIGN FOR THE TRAY GLUED TOGETHER FROM SECTIONS CUT FROM THE FIRST-GENERATION LAMINATE

Photo 29. SAWING HALF OF THE LAMINATE FOR THE COMPLETE TRAY DESIGN IN TWO EQUAL PARTS ON THE BAND SAW

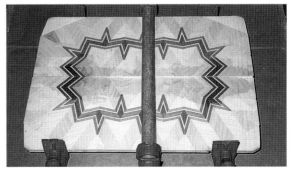

Photo 30. GLUING TOGETHER THE TWO HALVES OF THE LAMINATE FOR THE TRAY TO PRODUCE THE COMPLETE DESIGN FOR THE TRAY BOTTOM

Game Table

This project, a game table with a mitered laminate design on the top of the table, is not for the woodworker who is just learning how to make and manipulate laminates. It is a rather ambitious project, requiring considerable planning and time to construct. The most difficult part involves making three integrated mitered laminate designs to cover the entire top of the table. The three designs are all different standard designs. Around the outer edge of the top is a 30/50D square design. The circular design in the center of the tabletop is a 30/45A laminate. Between these two is an eight-sided 45/30A design. The three are fitted together so that laminate covers the entire table top. The primary wood in the table is walnut, but several other wood species were used in making the stripes. More conventional methods were used for making the remainder of the table—except for the braces on the legs.

The primary emphasis will be on planning and making the mitered laminates for the top; this will be discussed in greater detail than the construction of the remainder of the table. However, making and cutting the elliptical table braces will be discussed in some detail. Standard procedures are used in making all the mitered laminates. Refer to chapters 2, 3, and 4 for more detailed information on performing the various steps in the process. Information vital to accomplishing each step, such as the value of variables, will be given here. Photographs of every step in every process are not provided, but there are enough visual aids to help guide you through the various steps.

There are several distinct steps involved in making the table. Each step will be presented separately. The first step involves planning and sizing the designs so that they fit together into a harmonious and balanced design. The next step is making the mitered laminates so that they will fit into the overall plan. This involves making three different mitered laminates and converting each to a different type of connecting loop or configuration. The outer design is square, the middle one is eight-sided or octagonal, and the inner one is circular.

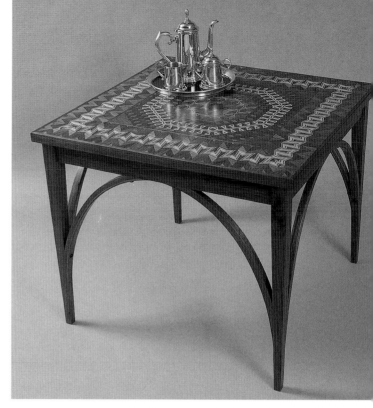

Project 5: GAME TABLE WITH MITERED LAMINATE TABLETOP; TABLETOP IS 35½ X 35½ INCHES (90 X 90 CM) AND THE TABLE STANDS 28½ INCHES (72.5 CM) TALL; WALNUT, CHERRY, MAPLE, BUBINGA, POPLAR, AND ONE UNKNOWN WOOD SPECIES.

Planning

Considerable planning is required to determine what areas should be occupied by the laminate designs and how these designs are made to properly fit into these areas. The design should be balanced with regard to size, configuration, and color. For balance, the length, width, and shape of each laminate must be defined. The wood species used for the stripes should blend with each other and with the wood used for the background (here, walnut). In order for the design to stand out, there must be a contrast between the background wood and the wood used for the stripes. Maple was chosen for some of the stripes. Cherry was used as a third component in one design. A species with distinct red overtones (bubinga) was used for one stripe in the smaller design in the middle of the table.

The configuration of the designs is an important consideration. A design that goes around the outer edges of the top is appropriate, because it frames in the entire top. This laminate was configured into a square.

A circular design is fitting for the center of a square area. (Actually the *circle* is an eight-sided figure.) The design appears to be circular, because the length of each side of the octagon is very short.

A third design is needed in between to tie the square and circle together. This design should be transitional, a step halfway between a square and a circle. One can think of it as *squaring a circle*, though it is probably easier to visualize the reverse process of *circling a square*. The first step is to cut off the four corners of the square. This results in an eight-sided figure and appears to be a logical place to discontinue the changeover from the square into a design for this area. A design in the shape of a regular octagon was thus chosen for the in-between laminate.

The structure of the table, with one exception, is conventional. I did not want this table to appear heavy or massive. Slim legs, however, would make the table unsteady or unstable. Rather than using stronger legs, I decided to use braced legs. Most braces, however, would get in the way of sitting at the table. This problem can be avoided if the braces are curved. The curve should be graceful and harmonious with the lines in the table, suggesting an oval-shaped or elliptically shaped brace, which would lend grace to the table and, at the same time, solve the sturdiness problem.

The Tabletop Design

Having chosen the configuration of the three designs for the tabletop, the size of each and their exact location should be the next considerations. The overall design should be balanced; no one design should dominate. The outline of each design is first sketched to scale (Figure 8). In the sketch, the areas representing the designs are shown in shades of gray.

I started out drawing a square area, an octagonal area, and a circular one. Then I changed any design area that seemed to be out of balance or harmony. Generally, balance seems to be better if the outer design width is somewhat larger and the center is smaller than the middle one. It may be necessary to adjust the space between the three areas, which should be about the same.

Selecting a specific design for each area is done in a similar fashion. The larger outer area should be made with a somewhat heavy, dense, or concentrated design. The center design should be airy, light, and more spread out.

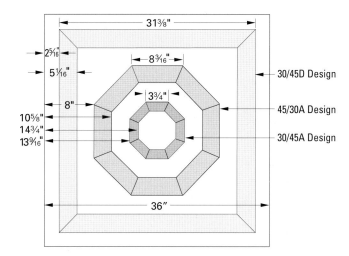

Figure 8. THE LOCATIONS (GRAY AREAS) OF THE THREE DESIGNS FOR THE TABLETOP

The octagonal design falls in between. After considering all the designs in chapter 4, I followed the above guidelines. I chose a 30/50D laminate for the design along the outer edge of the table, a 45/30A laminate for the octagonal configuration, and a 30/45A laminate for the inner circle.

The stripe should complement each design. A dense or compact design should be made with a wide, bold stripe. It is appropriate to use a multistrip stripe in this situation. It's fitting to use a few narrow strips along with a wide one. A five-strip stripe was chosen for the large square pattern. The stripe for the other two areas should be narrower and have fewer strips. The center design should have the narrowest stripe of the three. For the two inner stripes, three-strip stripes were selected.

Several variables must be calculated or determined before you are able to make a design that fills each gray-shaded area in the sketch (Figure 8). From the sketch, the height and total length of each design can be scaled. Several steps must be taken before a laminate can be made that meets these criteria. For a detailed discussion of sizing and dimensioning of standard mitered laminates, refer to chapter 9. *Note*: I have used inches through-out this section, but the same procedures can be used for metric measurements.

SQUARE LAMINATE DESIGN

Figure 8 was drawn to scale where 36 inches is the overall size of the table. The size of each element on the drawing can be determined by proportion regardless of the size of the drawing. Measure the length of the table in any units, then measure the length or width of any element on the drawing in the same units. For example, if the overall table measures 4 inches on the drawing, divide the actual length of the table by the length measured on the drawing, or 36 inches divided by 4 inches equals 9. The actual table is thus 9 times as long as the table on the drawing. Likewise, every element will be 9 times as long on the actual table as it is on the drawing. Thus, a part of the drawing that measures 2 inches is actually 2 inches times 9 or 18 inches long on the table.

As scaled from the drawing in Figure 8, the square laminate (30/50D) should be 2¾ inches wide. You will need a total length of 128 inches (4 sides x 32 inches, rounded off) of this design. As the initial step, a five-strip stripe for the design was selected.

The actual width of the stripe has a bearing on the width-to-height ratio of an RDU unit. I chose ⅝ inch as an approximate width for a design that is 2¾ inches wide. Draw a scaled model of a repeating design unit (RDU) of a 30/50D laminate with a ⅝-inch stripe. (Figure 9 depicts this RDU drawn with the actual stripe design, but this detail is not required to obtain the width to height ratio.) The width-to-height ratio (108 to 119) is 0.91. These values were measured by the computer. However, the measurements could also be made on the printed drawing itself, either in inches, centimeters, or any other unit. Each would give the same ratio. From this, calculate the width of an RDU by multiplying the desired height (2¾ inches) by this ratio. The calculation gives 2½ inches (2¾ inches x 0.91 ratio = 2½ inches) as the width of an RDU.

From the width of an RDU, calculate the number of units required for one side of the laminate. To do this, divide the maximum length of a side (31⅜ inches) by 2½ inches (see above). The result is 12.55. The actual number needed is the next whole number divisible by 2 or 14 RDUs required per side. Multiply 14 by 4 sides to get 56 as the total number of RDUs required for the entire laminate.

Review chapter 9 for the following calculations: There are two 30/50D laminate cross sections per one RDU. Thus, the number of the laminate sections needed is 56 times 2, or 112. From the latter number, it is easy to calculate the total number of linear laminate cross sections required. In the conversion process, it takes two

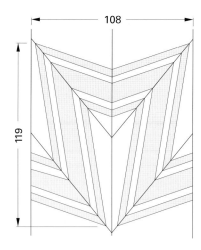

Figure 9. REPEATING DESIGN UNIT (RDU) FOR THE SQUARE LAMINATE FOR THE TABLETOP

linear laminate sections to make one 30/50D cross section. Thus, a total of 2 times 112, or 224, linear laminate cross sections must be obtainable from the linear laminate to provide adequate material for the entire design. There are, however, losses during the fabrication that must be considered; so add a 20% loss factor. This increases the number to 269.

From the number of linear laminate cross sections calculated above, determine the total length of linear laminate needed for the project. This requires two more calculations. First, determine how wide to cut the linear laminate so that the design will be 2¾ inches wide. Use equation 8 in chapter 9 (page 89) for this calculation. Add the width of a 30/50D cross section (half the width of an RDU or 1¼ inches) to the width of a saw kerf (⅛ inch, here—use the actual width of the kerf cut by your saw). Divide this sum by twice the sine of the angle used for cutting the 30/50D laminate (50°). This calculation gives ⅞ inch as the width to cut the cross sections from the linear laminate.

What length of linear laminate is used up for every ⅞-inch-wide cross section that is cut off at 30°? This value can be calculated from equation 4, chapter 9 (see page 88). Add the width of a cutoff cross section (⅞ inch) to the width of a saw kerf (⅛ inch). Divide this by the sine of the cutting angle (30°). This gives 2 inches as the length of linear laminate needed for each cross section cut. With this number, the total length of linear laminate required can be determined. Multiply the total number of linear laminate cross sections needed (269) by 2 inches to get 538 inches of linear laminate that must be made for the project.

The first step in the fabrication process is to make the linear laminate. To decrease the amount of work needed to make a mitered laminate, make the linear laminate twice as thick as is needed for the final design. It can then be sawed in half, thus doubling the length of laminate produced. Instead of needing 538 inches of linear laminate, it is necessary to make only half (269 inches) of this amount. Cut 269 inches or about 23 feet of each wood for the stripe and double this length for the sideboards. Cut all pieces ¾ inch wide. Make one maple strip ¼ inch thick and two ³⁄₃₂ inch thick. Cut two walnut strips ³⁄₃₂ inch thick. Cut the walnut sideboards 2½ inches by ¾ inch. Position a walnut strip on either side of the ¼-inch maple strip. Sandwich this between two strips of ³⁄₃₂-inch maple. This is the stripe. Place the walnut sideboards on either side of the stripe. Glue these together, clamp, and allow to dry thoroughly. The linear laminate is pictured on the left side of the sliding table jig in Photo 31.

The above information provides all you need to make a second-generation mitered laminate (30/50D design) 2¾ inches wide—enough to go around the outside border of the table. The design factors for this laminate and the two to follow are summarized in Table 1. Cut ⅞-inch-wide cross sections at 30° from this laminate, using the sliding table cutoff jig. Standard procedures are used in the fabrication of this laminate. Photo 31 shows this cutting operation. Turn alternate sections over and glue them into a matching zigzag pattern. This produces a first-generation laminate. Trim and sand the laminate.

Attach a positioning jig to the sliding table jig. Cut the above laminate at 50° through the centers of the descending legs (D-points). Turn alternate cross sections upside-down and glue them together into a second-generation laminate. See Photo 32 for the cutting procedure and Photo 33 for the clamping operation. Trim and sand the glued-up sections. This is the laminate that is used for the border design.

From this laminate, cut mitered sections the length of the table. Set the angle fence at 45°. Position the laminate against the fence so that the saw cut will go through a central point on the design. Either an A-point or a D-point can be selected. Miter one end of the laminate. Turn the laminate over and cut a second miter on the other end of the side. This cut must go through the same central point for the stripe to match at the mitered cuts.

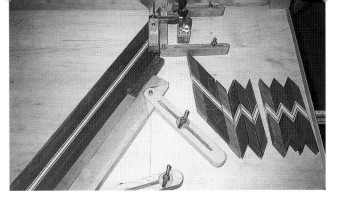

Photo 31. HOW THE LINEAR LAMINATE FOR THE SQUARE TABLE DESIGN IS CUT INTO CROSS SECTIONS TO MAKE A FIRST-GENERATION DESIGN

DESIGN FACTOR	IDENTITY OF THE DESIGN		
	30/50D	45/30A	30/45A
No. of sides	4	8	Circle
Width of design, in.	2-3/4	2-5/8	1-3/16
Total length of design, in.	32(128)	8-3/16(67)	3-3/4(32)
Width of stripe, in.	5/8	7/16	5/16
Width/height ratio	0.91	0.45	1.45
Width of RDU, in.	2-1/2	1-3/16	2
Calc. number, RDU's/side	12.55	6.9	1.88
Actual number RDU's used for calc.	14(56)	8(64)	2(16)
No. second-generation laminates	112	128	32
No. linear laminate x-sections	224	256	64
No. linear laminate x-section + 20%	269	307	77
Width, linear laminate x-section, in.	7/8	23/32	25/32
Length, linear laminate /x-section, in.	2	1-3/8	1-13/16
Total length linear laminate needed, in.	538	421	140
Length, linear laminate to make, in.	269	211	70
Width, center stripe, in.	1/4	3/16	3/16
Width, center stripe next to center, in.	3/32	1/8	1/16
Width, stripe next to above, in.	3/32	—	—
Width, outboard plank, in.	2-1/2	2-1/2	2-1/2
Wood in center stripe	maple	cherry	bubinga
Wood in stripe next to center	walnut	maple	maple
Wood in stripe next to above	maple	—	—
Wood in outboard plank	walnut	walnut	walnut

Table 1. SUMMARY OF DESIGN FACTORS FOR GAME TABLE

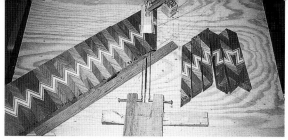

Photo 32. CUTTING THE FIRST-GENERATION LAMINATE INTO CROSS SECTIONS FOR A SECOND-GENERATION DESIGN

Photo 33. HOW THE CROSS SECTIONS CUT FROM THE FIRST-GENERATION LAMINATE ARE ARRANGED AND GLUED TO PRODUCE A SECOND-GENERATION DESIGN

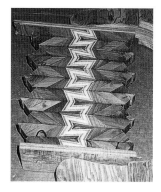

Photo 34. CUTTING A 45° MITER ON ONE END OF THE SECOND-GENERATION LAMINATE SO THE DESIGN CAN BE MATCHED TO A SIMILARLY CUT PIECE OF LAMINATE TO PRODUCE A 90° CORNER

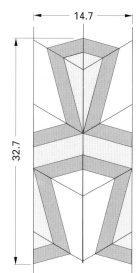

Figure 10. REPEATING DESIGN UNIT (RDU) FOR THE OCTAGONAL DESIGN FOR THE TABLETOP

Cut off approximately 31⅜ inches of the laminate measured at its longest point. Photo 34 shows the cutting operation. The laminate will probably not be exactly this length, but choose a central point that is the closest to this measurement. Cut a second side from the mitered laminate to the same length. Having made a linear laminate that is double the required thickness, cut each mitered side into two halves of equal width. Sand the faces of the four sides until they are smooth and planar.

Arrange the four sides into a square and clamp them together, matching the stripe at the four miters. This laminate will be used as a pattern to mark the octagonal design so that the two will fit together properly. Mark the inside edges of the four segments for trimming. The marks must be parallel to the design and must match up at each corner of the miter. Only the minimum amount of material should be trimmed off so as to leave the laminate as wide as possible. Trim each sector along these lines. This should result in a configuration with a true inner square. Glue the four segments together, matching the stripes on the two sides of the glue lines. Put this configuration aside until the other two laminates have been completed.

OCTAGONAL LAMINATE DESIGN

The octagonal laminate design is made with a three-strip stripe and is somewhat narrower than the square laminate. Based on Figure 8, the design should be 2⅝ inches wide with eight mitered sides, each a little over 8 inches long.

The steps in the sizing of this laminate are the same as for the square laminate. The width of the stripe chosen for this design is ⁷⁄₁₆ inch. Draw a model of a repeating design unit (RDU) for a 45/30A laminate with a ⁷⁄₁₆-inch stripe (Figure 10). Based on the drawing, the width-to-height ratio (14.7 to 32.7) is 0.45. Calculate the width of an RDU (2⅝ inches x 0.45 = 1³⁄₁₆ inches).

To determine the number of RDUs needed per side of laminate, divide the length of a side (8³⁄₁₆ inches from Figure 8) by the width of an RDU (1³⁄₁₆ inches). The calculation gives 6.9 RDUs, but, for the purpose of making this calculation, assume that it will require 8, the next even whole number. For the entire laminate, multiply the number of RDUs per side (8) by the number of sides (8). The result is 64. Double this number to 128 for the number of 45/30A cross sections needed. Again, double the number to determine the number of cross sections that have to be cut from a linear laminate. Two times 128, or 256, is the number of linear laminate sections needed for the project. Apply a 20% loss factor, giving 307 as the total number of cross sections that need to be cut from the linear laminate.

Calculating the length of linear laminate needed for the project requires one additional value: how wide to cut the cross sections from the linear laminate so that the design will be 2⅝ inches wide and long enough to make all the eight sectors of the eight-sided figure. Use equation 8, chapter 9 (page 89) for this calculation. Add half of the width of an RDU (1³⁄₁₆ inches divided by 2) to the saw-blade kerf width (⅛ inch). Divide this value (²³⁄₃₂ inch) by twice the sine of the last cutting angle (30°). The result is ²³⁄₃₂ inch. This should result in a 45/30A laminate of the desired width of 2⅝ inches.

With this number, the length of linear laminate needed per linear laminate cross section can be calculated (see equation 4, chapter 9, page 88). Add the width of a linear laminate cross section (²³⁄₃₂ inch) to the width of a saw kerf (⅛ inch), and divide this sum by the sine of the cutting angle (45°). The result is 1⅜ inches as the length of linear laminate required for every linear laminate section. Multiply this value by the total number of sections needed (307) to obtain 421 inches as the total length of linear laminate required for the project.

The only other design variables that are needed are the composition and size of the strips in the stripe and the size and wood species to be used for the outboard planks. Cut the center cherry strips ³⁄₁₆ inch thick and ¾ inch wide. Make two maple strips, ⅛ inch thick and the same width as the cherry strips. Then cut two pieces of walnut, 2½ inches wide and ¾ inch thick. Glue these five pieces together, placing the cherry in the center, a maple strip on each side of the cherry, then all of these strips between the two pieces of walnut. The stripe should thus be ⁷⁄₁₆ inch wide, and the linear laminate measures 5⁷⁄₁₆ inches wide by ¾ inch thick. Since the width of the laminate is wide enough to be cut in half, make it half of 421 inches or 211 inches long.

Cut this linear laminate into cross sections ²³⁄₃₂ inch wide at 45° (Photo 35). Glue these into a first-generation laminate (Photo 36), first turning every other section upside-down. To convert this to a second-generation design, cut the above design through the A-points at 30° (Photo 37). Glue these sections into a 45/30A laminate design (Photo 38), but do not make any longer than the capacity of your

Photo 35. CUTTING THE LINEAR LAMINATE FOR THE OCTAG-ONAL DESIGN FOR THE GAME TABLE INTO CROSS SECTIONS FROM WHICH A FIRST-GENERATION DESIGN IS MADE

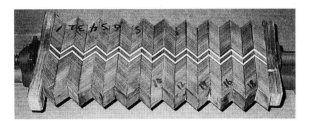

Photo 36. GLUE-UP OF THE FIRST-GENERATION LAMINATE MADE FROM SECTIONS CUT FROM THE LINEAR LAMINATE

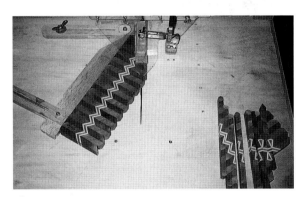

Photo 37. THE FIRST-GENERATION LAMINATE IS CUT INTO CROSS SECTIONS THAT CAN BE GLUED TOGETHER TO MAKE A SECOND-GENERATION DESIGN.

Photo 38. THE SECOND-GENERATION LAMINATE IS GLUED-UP FROM CROSS SECTIONS CUT FROM A FIRST-GENERATION DESIGN.

Photo 39. THE SECOND-GENERATION DESIGN IS CUT INTO TWO HALVES ON THE BAND SAW.

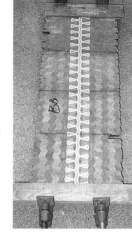

Photo 40. FOUR HALVED SECTIONS OF LAMINATE ARE GLUED TOGETHER INTO A LONGER SECOND-GENERATION DESIGN.

band saw. In the clamping operation shown, there is no glue between the two center sections. Trim and sand both sides of each section until planar. Cut each of these sections into halves (Photo 39) and sand. Glue the halved laminate sections together into a linear configuration as shown in Photo 40.

Next, convert the linear design into eight segments for an octagonal configuration. Miter one end of this laminate at an angle of 22½° through either an A-point or a D-point. Turn the laminate over and cut off a piece at the same angle and through the same central point. Make the overall length of the cutoff piece as close to 8³⁄₁₆ inches as possible. This should require about 8 RDUs. Again, turn the laminate over and cut off a

Photo 41. CUTTING A 22½° MITER ON ONE END OF A SECTION OF A SECOND-GENERATION LAMINATE. AFTER MITERING BOTH ENDS, EIGHT OF THESE SECTIONS GLUED TOGETHER PRODUCE AN OCTAGONAL CONFIGURATION.

second sector of the same length. Repeat (Photo 41), cutting off a total of eight identical mitered pieces.

Arrange these into an eight-sided figure; but before gluing them, clamp them together, matching the stripe all the way around. Mark each sector along its inner edge prior to trimming it. Mark them so the adjacent edges match up at each mitered corner and all edges run parallel to the design. Trim each sector at the mark, then glue them together. This will be used as a pattern with which to mark the circular laminate so that both sections will fit into an overall pattern. Sand both faces of this octagonal laminate and put aside until the next and last mitered laminate has been made.

THE CIRCULAR LAMINATE DESIGN

The procedures for making this laminate are the same as for making the other laminates. However, different variables apply. It is necessary to designate the overall dimensions of the stripe before proceeding. The overall width of the stripe is ⁵⁄₁₆ inch. As shown in Figure 8, the circular center design should be 1³⁄₁₆ inches wide. Make a scale drawing of an RDU of this 30/45A laminate (Figure 11). The width-to-height ratio (49.1 to 33.9) is 1.45. Multiply this ratio by the height (1⅜ inches) of an RDU. This gives 2 inches as the width of an RDU. A 30/45A cross section is half of this width or 1 inch.

With this value for the width of a 30/45A cross section, the width of a linear laminate cross section can be calculated, using equation 8 in chapter 9 (page 89). Divide the sum of the width of the second-generation cross section (1 inch) and the saw kerf (⅛ inch) by twice the sine of the cutting angle (45°) for the 30/45A laminate. The result is ²⁵⁄₃₂ inch. Cut all linear laminate cross sections to this width.

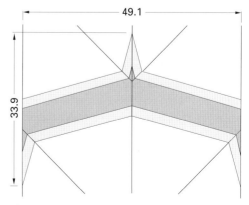

Figure 11. REPEATING DESIGN UNIT (RDU) FOR THE CIRCULAR DESIGN FOR THE TABLETOP

The only other factor that must be calculated before fabrication can start is the total length of the linear laminate required for the project. This requires several calculations. Start by determining the number of RDUs required for the design. Using Figure 8, scale the length of a segment of the circular design at its widest point. This is 3¾ inches. Divide this value by the width of an RDU (2 inches). The answer is 1.88, but use 2 because it is the next even whole number. For eight sides, the requirement becomes 16; this is the number of RDUs needed for the entire design. This translates to thirty-two 30/45A cross sections or 64 linear laminate cross sections. Apply a loss factor of 20% by multiplying this number by 1.20. Thus, you will need 77 linear laminate cross sections.

The next step is to calculate the length of linear laminate used up in cutting a cross section. Apply equation 4, chapter 9, page 88. Use the following values in the equation: 25/32-inch width of cross section; ⅛-inch width of saw kerf; 30° cutting angle. Thus, 1 13/16 inches of linear laminate are required for each cross section. For 77 sections, multiply this value by 1 13/16 inches. Thus, a total of 140 inches of linear laminate is required for this laminate.

This completes the calculations. The linear laminate is made from the following: a 3/16-inch-thick strip of bubinga; a 1/16-inch-thick strip of maple on each side of the bubinga; and a piece of walnut, 2½ inches wide by ¾ inch thick, which make up the outboard planks on either side of the stripe. The strips for the stripe are cut ¾ inch wide. Make each of these five pieces of wood about 6 feet long, then glue the pieces together. This should be an adequate amount of linear laminate for the project (140 inches/2 = 70 inches or about 6 feet), since the 30/45A will be cut into two halves just before the laminate is glued into an eight-sided figure.

Follow standard procedures when making the 30/45A laminate design. Cut the linear laminate at 30° into 25/32-inch-wide cross sections. Glue these into a first-generation laminate. Convert this design to a 30/45A laminate by cutting it at 45° through the A-points (Photo 42). Glue these sections together into a second-generation design. Trim and sand, according to the usual procedures.

Cut from this laminate four segments at 22½°, each two RDUs long, through either the A-points or the D-points (Photo 43). Glue these four segments together into a semicircular arrangement. Cut this into two halves on a band saw, and glue the two halves together to form a circular design. Sand both faces of the circular laminate. Refer to the clock

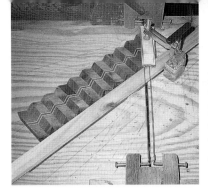

Photo 42. CUTTING THE FIRST-GENERATION LAMINATE FOR THE CIRCULAR DESIGN FOR THE GAME TABLE INTO CROSS SECTIONS AT 45°

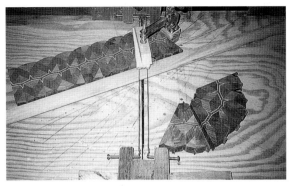

Photo 43. CUTTING A SECOND-GENERATION LAMINATE AT 22½° INTO SEGMENTS SO THAT EIGHT WILL FIT TOGETHER INTO A CIRCLE. THREE OF THE SEGMENTS HAVE BEEN PLACED TOGETHER AT THE LOWER RIGHT PART OF THE PHOTO TO ILLUSTRATE HOW THEY FIT INTO PART OF A CIRCULAR DESIGN.

project (page 124) for more details on the procedure for converting a laminate into a circular configuration.

There will probably be a jagged hole in the center of this design that must be filled in. Cut a round hole in the center of the design just large enough to remove all the sharp points, leaving the opening round and smooth. Make a circular piece of walnut (the thickness of the laminate) to fit snugly inside this hole. Glue it in place and sand both sides of the laminate until the surfaces are even and smooth.

Assembling the Tabletop

The three laminates are now ready to be fitted together. Center the octagonal laminate on top of the circular center design. The two laminates should overlap all the way around, leaving no area where there is no wood. Mark the circular laminate along the inside edges of the eight-sided figure. Cut off the overlapping wood from the central design along these marks. The eight-sided center laminate should then fit inside the octagonal hole in the larger eight-sided figure.

Fit the outer square and the middle laminate in the same way. Center the square laminate on top of the octagonal design. The two will probably not overlap close to the corners of the square. However, mark the middle laminate, using the inner edges of the square laminate as a guide. Trim the octagonal laminate along these marks. The two laminates should now fit, one inside the other, except for the four corners between the square and octagonal laminates where there are triangular holes. These areas must be filled in, converting the octagon outline into a square.

First, mark the uncut edges on the octagonal design for trimming. The marks must be straight, parallel to the opposite edge of each sector, and all edges of the octagon must be the same length. Trim the four sides on these marks. This should produce a regular octagon. Glue a triangular piece of walnut to each edge that has just been trimmed. The walnut should be the same thickness as the laminate and the triangle should be somewhat larger than the area to be filled. After the glue has dried, trim the edges of the triangles flush with the edges that were fitted to the inside of the square laminate. This configuration should now fit inside and completely fill the square design. Sand both surfaces of the octagonal design. The three laminates should now all fit together.

The three laminates should be glued to a piece of plywood for added strength and stability. Cut a piece of ⅜-inch- or ½-inch-thick plywood into a square as large as the outside dimensions of the outer laminate. A good grade of plywood, such as Baltic birch, should be used. Glue the square laminate design to the plywood, adjusting its position so that it is flush with the outside edges of the plywood. Next, glue the octagonal design onto the plywood and inside of the square laminate. Then glue the circular laminate inside the hole in the octagonal laminate. Trim, square, and sand the four edges of the top. Glue four strips of walnut that are ³⁄₁₆ inch thick and as wide as the thickness of the laminate plus plywood around the edges. Miter the corners before they are glued on.

There will be small cracks rather than tight joints where the three laminates join. To fix this, route a dado ⅛ inch wide and ¼ inch deep along all the joints where the laminates come together. Glue walnut strips having the same dimensions as the dado into these areas. Sand the entire top until it is even and planar.

Constructing the Table

The remainder of the table is constructed of walnut. Except for the leg braces, conventional methods and procedures are used. These will not be detailed. The legs and rails are constructed with mortise and tenon joints. Cut the legs 27½ inches long and 1⅞ inches square at the top. Taper two adjoining faces, starting 3 inches from the top, to a 1-inch square at the bottom. Make the rails 2¾ inches wide and ¾ inch thick. Cut the rails so that the distance between the shoulders on the tenons is 5½ inches shorter than the outside dimensions of the top of the table. Glue the legs to the rails and attach conventional braces at the corners where the rails join the legs.

Making elliptical braces for the table legs is not common and the process will be discussed in some detail. Each elliptical brace goes from the center of the rail to within 3 inches of the bottom of the leg. The major and minor axes for the inner ellipse are 22¼ inches and half of the distance between the legs, respectively (Figure 12). The axes for the outer face of a brace are ¾ inch longer to account for the ¾-inch thickness of the brace. The braces are made of thin strips of walnut. The glued strips are clamped between two cauls, one shaped like the outside quadrant of an ellipse and the other like the inside.

The first step is making the shaped cauls, as shown in Photo 44. Make the cauls from a piece of 2 x 8 or 2 x 10 about 30 inches long. Draw two ellipses on the board (Figure 13). The ellipses can be drawn directly onto the board to be used for the cauls, or they can be drawn on a piece of countertop laminate (Figure 14) where the area between the ellipses is cut out and used as a pattern on the board to be made into cauls. One is a pattern for the inside of the curve and the other is for the outside. The inside ellipse has major and minor axes of 22¼ inches and half the distance between the legs, respectively, as shown in Figure 13. For the outer one, these values are 23 inches and half the distance between the legs plus ¾ inch.

After marking the ellipses on the 2 x 8 or 2 x 10, cut the board along these marks. The cauls are used between clamps. Having made the cauls, the elliptical braces can be made. Make six walnut strips ⅛ inch thick, 1 inch wide, and about 33 inches long. Place the glued strips between the cauls and apply pressure with clamps to force the strips of walnut into the shape of the cauls. Photo 44 shows a brace clamped in the cauls. After the glue has dried, the bonded strips will retain the shape of the cauls.

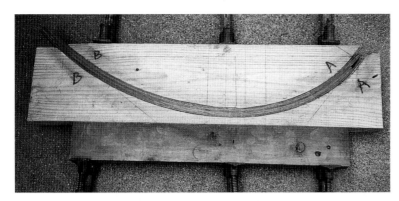

Photo 44. A CURVED BRACE BEING GLUED TOGETHER FROM THIN STRIPS OF WOOD WHILE BEING CLAMPED TOGETHER WITH CAULS

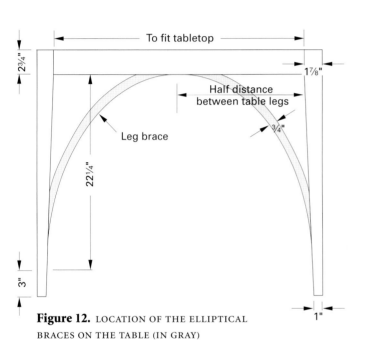

Figure 12. LOCATION OF THE ELLIPTICAL BRACES ON THE TABLE (IN GRAY)

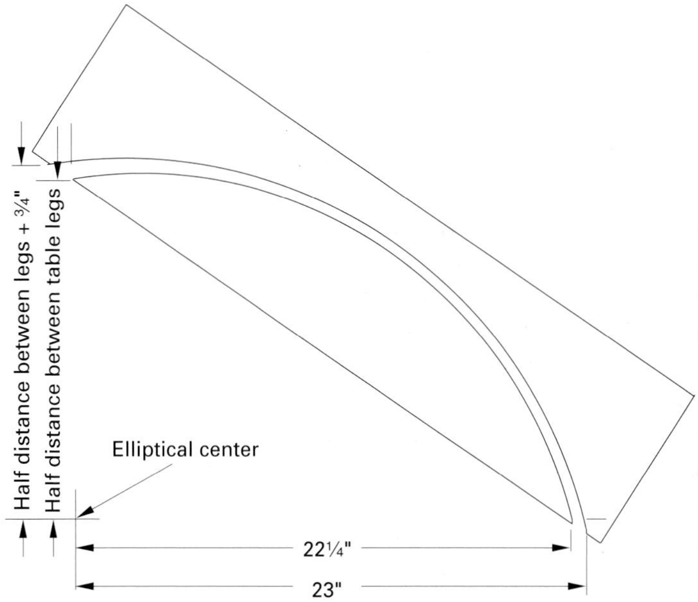

Figure 13. BASIS FOR DRAWING ELLIPTICAL ARCS ON CAULS

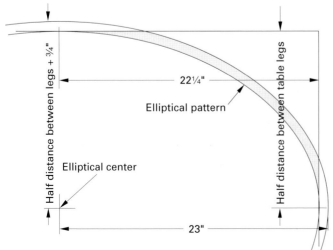

Figure 14. BASIS FOR DRAWING ELLIPTICAL PATTERN FOR BRACE

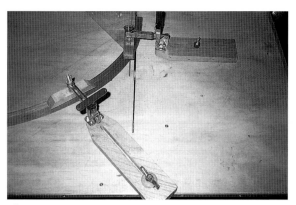

Photo 45. A CURVED BRACE CLAMPED TO THE SLIDING
TABLE CUTOFF JIG, HAVING AN END MITERED TO FIT
BETWEEN A LEG AND RAIL OF THE TABLE

Plane or joint both edges of the brace until it is ¾ inch
thick. Make a total of eight of these braces.

The next step is to cut off or miter both ends of
each brace so that it fits in the area between a leg and a
rail as shown in the drawing in Figure 12. I used the sliding cutoff jig along with the left half of the scribed-line
jig to make the miter cuts on either end of the brace. See
Photo 45. The edge of the positioning jig is used to indicate where the cut will be made. Adjust this jig so that
one edge of the clear plastic sheeting is parallel to the
saw blade and almost touching the blade.

Either of two methods can be used for positioning
the brace for cutting. The brace can be marked on each
end where the cut needs to be made. Then the brace is
positioned so that the edge of the clear plastic sheeting
is parallel to and just on the mark on the brace.

An alternative way to position the brace is based on
the leg and rail dimensions shown in Figure 14. Use the
inside dimensions. After it has been accurately positioned, clamp in two places as demonstrated in Photo 45.
Cut off one end of the brace. Unclamp it, turn it around,
and miter the other end, using the same technique. It
should now fit between a leg and a rail. Miter both ends
of all eight braces.

Next, the mitered braces are attached to the table.
Clamp one end of the brace to a rail and the other end
to a leg. The outside surfaces should be flush with both
the rail and the leg. Drill a hole for a screw through the
brace and into the rail. Drill a second hole through the
brace and into a leg. Countersink both holes on the brace
to accommodate the head of the screw. Apply glue to
the mating surfaces, and firmly screw the brace to the
rail and leg. Glue a plug into each screw hole. Repeat
this procedure for the other seven braces.

This completes the construction of the table except
for attaching the top to the leg assembly. The top is centered on the rails and fastened by some conventional
method to the rails. For the table in Photo 46, I used
metal tabletop fasteners. I routed a ¼-inch-square groove
along the inside surface of the four railings, ½ inch from
the top. Then, I centered the top of the table over the
railing square and screwed two metal tabletop fasteners
to the underside and along each edge of the top so that
one end of each fastener protruded into the groove of a
railing. Sand the table. Complete the table by applying
your favorite finish.

Photo 46.
DETAIL OF
TABLETOP

Glossary

A-design—The design formed by gluing together cross sections that were obtained by cutting through the A-points of a prior-generation laminate.

A-laminate—The mitered laminate made by gluing together cross sections that were obtained by cutting through the A-points of a prior-generation laminate.

A-point—The central point of the design in a crosscut section where the major part of the design changes from the area below the longitudinal axis to the area above as viewed from left to right.

AD-design—The design formed by gluing together cross sections that were obtained by cutting through both the A-points and the D-points of a prior-generation laminate.

AD-laminate—The mitered laminate made by gluing together cross sections that were obtained by cutting through both the A-points and the D-points of a prior-generation laminate.

central point—The location on the longitudinal axis and on the leg of the design that is midway between the cut faces of the cross section, where the design to the left is an inverse mirror image of the design to the right.

connected stripe—A mitered laminate where the stripe in each crosscut section coincides with or matches the stripe at the glue line in the two adjoining cross sections.

continuous stripe—See connected stripe.

corresponding points—Any pair of points on a mitered laminate design that are located equidistant and in opposite directions from a central point where one point is an inverse mirror image of the other point as viewed from the central point.

crosscut section—A narrow, parallel-sided strip of wood cut diagonally from a board or laminate that is used to make mitered laminates.

cross section—See crosscut section.

design unit—Part of a mitered laminate design made up of two adjacent cross sections where one section is an inverse mirror image of the other.

D-design—The design formed by gluing together cross sections that were obtained by cutting through the D-points of a prior-generation laminate.

D-laminate—The mitered laminate made by gluing together cross sections that were obtained by cutting through the D-points of a prior-generation laminate.

D-point—The central point in the design in a cross section where the major part of the design changes from the area above the longitudinal axis to the area below as viewed from left to right.

enhanced design—A mitered laminate design that was made with a continuous or connected stripe.

enhanced laminate—See enhanced mitered laminate.

enhanced mitered laminate—A mitered laminate that was made with a continuous or connected stripe.

first-generation design—The design obtained when cross sections cut from a standard linear laminate are glued together according to the standard procedure.

first-generation mitered laminate—The laminate obtained when cross sections cut from a standard linear laminate are glued together according to the standard procedure.

first-generation process—The process of converting a linear laminate to a first-generation mitered laminate according to the standard procedure.

fourth-generation design—The design obtained when cross sections cut from a third-generation mitered laminate are glued together according to the standard procedure.

fourth-generation mitered laminate—The laminate obtained when cross sections cut from a third-generation mitered laminate are glued together according to the standard procedure.

fourth-generation process—The process of converting a third-generation mitered laminate into a fourth-generation mitered laminate according to the standard procedure.

laminate—A composite of different mitered shapes and varieties of wood glued together in layers, blocks, or tiers into a design or pattern.

linear laminate—A composite of one or more strips of wood (the stripe) glued between two boards or planks (outboard planks).

linear mitered laminate—A planar mitered laminate where the design runs in a straight line along its longitudinal axis.

mitered laminate—A composite of small mitered blocks of wood obtained by cutting a laminate into parallel-sided cross sections that are glued back together into a different configuration.

next-generation laminate—The mitered laminate obtained when a laminate is cut into cross sections and reglued into a different design.

nonstandard design—A design obtained by a process where at least one step in the standard procedure is not followed.

nonstandard mitered laminate—A laminate made by a process where at least one step in the standard procedure is not followed.

nonstandard pattern—See nonstandard design.

nonstandard process—The process of making a mitered laminate where at least one step in the standard procedure is not followed.

nonstandard stripe—A stripe that is not made according to the standard procedure.

nonsymmetrical stripe—See nonstandard stripe.

outboard planks—The boards in a linear laminate that are glued to opposite sides of the stripe.

planar mitered laminate—A mitered laminate in which the entire design is in one plane.

prior-generation laminate—The laminate that was converted to the next-generation mitered laminate.

repeating design unit—See design unit.

RDU—See design unit.

Glossary (continued)

second-generation design—The design obtained when cross sections cut from a first-generation mitered laminate are glued together according to the standard procedure.

second-generation mitered laminate—The laminate obtained when cross sections cut from a first-generation mitered laminate are glued together according to the standard procedure.

second-generation process—The process of converting a first-generation mitered laminate to a second-generation mitered laminate according to the standard procedure.

section—See crosscut section.

standard design—The design made when a standard laminate is converted to the next-generation laminate according to the standard procedure.

standard mitered laminate—A laminate made from a standard linear laminate by processes in which all standard procedures are followed.

standard process—The process of making a mitered laminate in which all steps in the conversion of one laminate to the next-generation mitered laminate follow a specific set of rules.

standard stripe—A laminated composite of an unequal number of strips of wood glued together that are symmetrical with respect to its longitudinal axis.

stripe—A composite of one or more narrow strips of wood glued between two boards (outboard planks).

symmetrical stripe—See standard stripe.

third-generation design—The design obtained when cross sections cut from a second-generation mitered laminate are glued together according to the standard procedure.

third-generation mitered laminate—The laminate obtained when cross sections cut from a second-generation mitered laminate are glued together according to the standard procedure.

third-generation process—The process of converting a second-generation mitered laminate to a third-generation mitered laminate according to the standard procedure.

variable factors—Procedures or conditions in the standard process that can be changed or modified during the production of a mitered laminate.

Index